Susan Fox

Weimaraners

Everything About Housing, Care, Nutrition, Breeding, and Health Care

Filled with Full-color Photographs

Illustrations by Michele Earle-Bridges

BARRON'S

2 CONTENTS

History and Origin of the Breed   5

Early Origins   5

A Versatile Breed   8

The Weimaraner Arrives Stateside   9

The Weimaraner Club of America   11

As a Hunter   11

The Weimaraner Standard   11

Understanding Your Weimaraner   17

About Purebred Dogs   17

Is the Weimaraner the Right Dog for You?   18

Part of the Family   18

Exercise   18

Obedience Training   19

Male or Female?   22

More than One Puppy?   23

Selecting a Weimaraner   25

Should You Own a Dog?   25

The Modern Dog   25

Where to Buy Your Weimaraner   27

Types   28

Important Papers   30

What to Look for in a Healthy Weimaraner   30

Care of the Weimaraner Puppy   33

Equipment   33

To the Veterinarian   37

The First Few Nights   37

Safety Considerations   38

Life with a Puppy   39

Car Travel   40

HOW-TO: Housetraining   42

Training   45

Why?   45

The Leader   45

When to Begin Training   46

Aversion Tools   47

Positive Reinforcement   47

A Consistent Standard   48

Training Equipment   49

Value of Obedience Classes   49

Basic Obedience Commands   50

Other Useful Commands   54

Socialization   55

Care of the Adult Weimaraner   57

Routine   57

Exercising Your Dog   57

Behavior Problems   57

A Word on Breeding   59

Spaying and Neutering   59

Toys and Bones   59

Boarding Kennels   60

Air Travel   60

The Senior Dog   61

Saying Good-bye   61

HOW-TO: Grooming   62

Feeding	65
What's in that Food?	65
Types of Food	65
What to Feed	67
How Much to Feed	68
When to Feed	70
Drinking Water	71
Food and Water Dishes	71
Supplements, Table Scraps, and Treats	71

Common Ailments and Medical Problems	73
Pet Health Insurance	73
External Parasites	73
Internal Parasites	75
Immunizations	77
Other Conditions	79
Bloat	79
Hip Dysplasia	80

Hypertrophic Osteodystrophy	82
Hypothyroidism	82
Skin Problems	82
Lumps and Bumps	83
Snake Bite	83

Sharing Your Life with a Weimaraner	85
Field Trials	85
AKC Hunting Tests	86
Weimaraner Club of America Shooting and Retrieving Ratings	86
Obedience Trials and Titles	86
Canine Good Citizenship	87
Showing Your Weimaraner	87
Therapy Dogs	88
Agility	90
Tracking	91
Search and Rescue	91
Flyball	91

Information	92
Index	94

HISTORY AND ORIGIN OF THE BREED

The Weimaraner (pronounced either "VYE-mar-ahner" or "WYE-mar-honor") is a large, striking gray dog developed as a hunting dog and companion for German nobility. Originally owned by a select group, the Weimaraner was not kept or sold as a pet. Today, when not competing for field, show, or obedience titles, the Weimaraner is most often found as a loving family pet.

The Weimaraner is classified as one of the Versatile or Continental Breeds. These breeds were imported from continental Europe, primarily during the early twentieth century, and include the Brittany, German Shorthaired Pointer, German Wirehaired Pointer, Vizsla, and Weimaraner. Continental Breeds all have docked tails. The Weimaraner is the largest and most powerful member of this group. The Versatile Breeds are so called, because these sporting dogs were developed to point upland birds and waterfowl as well as to hunt furred game.

Many people are attracted to the Weimaraner's elegant looks, which have been depicted in photographs and books by the famous photographer William Wegman. Wegman photographs the dogs in a variety of

The Weimaraner is the largest member of the sporting dog family, but it can make a great family pet.

unusual poses—noble, silly, calm, and stoic— and also as anthropomorphic characters in fairy tales. These images have focused attention on the breed and increased people's interest in owning a Weimaraner. It is important to note, however, that although Weimaraners can be noble and silly, they are rarely calm and stoic. Do not be mistaken about the character of the Weimaraner based on Wegman's photographs; his models are highly trained, disciplined dogs.

Early Origins

The Weimaraner's early history is hard to trace. As is true of many breeds, the exact origins are unknown. Weimaraners are thought to be an old breed and may have existed as far back as the seventeenth century. A 1632 painting of Prince Rupert of the Palatinate by Anthony Van Dyck depicts the prince posing next to a silver-gray dog similar in color and size to a Weimaraner. Silver-gray dogs are depicted in paintings, tapestries, woodcuts, and sculptures dating from the twelfth century. One of the more interesting tapestries from medieval times features dogs resembling modern Weimaraners surrounding a captured unicorn. While it is unlikely these ancient gray dogs were Weimaraners as the breed is presently known, it is possible that they are the breed's ancestors.

The dogs have many features that typify the modern Weimaraner, including a thin, high-set ear and a deep line down the middle of the head.

Fanciers of the breed have traced the Weimaraner back to several potential hound ancestors. A frequently cited theory is that the Weimaraner was a mutation from the St. Hubertus Branchen. This breed of hound is now extinct, but it is thought to be the master strain of hunting dogs from which all other types descended. The Branchen hounds were black with red or fawn marks over their eyes and on their legs and with occasional small white marks on the chest. Scientists know that two black animals can produce a gray one. The Weimaraner's silver-gray color is believed to be a mutation from the black color of the St. Hubertus Branchen. Like those of the Branchen, the occurrence of reddish-yellow markings on the legs and above the eyes is described in a proposed 1949 Weimaraner Breed Standard revision. Most often referred to as "dobe markings," these marks occasionally still appear in modern Weimaraners. Another potential hound ancestor is the red Schweisshund, a scent and tracking dog descended from the Bloodhound. The Bloodhound in turn is believed to have directly descended from the St. Hubertus Branchen.

Other research traces possible early ancestors of the Weimaraner to the gray hunting hounds of King Louis IX in the thirteenth century French Court. Known as the Chien Gris de Saint Louis, or the Gray Hound of Saint Louis, the breed was originally from Egypt. Around 1248, King Louis became familiar with the gray hounds while in Egypt during the Crusades. According to one account, the king hunted gazelle with the gray dogs in the Holy Land. He later obtained a pack of these dogs. Several breeds of dogs were developed from the king's hounds, each for a specific type of hunting. In fact, these dogs may have been the animals depicted in the twelfth century art referred to earlier.

Because the color gray is genetically recessive, it indicates selective breeding. German breeders raised the gray hound dogs in the state of Thuringia near Weimar, in central Germany. Because of the locale, the breed became known as Weimar Pointers (*Vorstehhund* in German) or Weimaraners.

Discounted Theories of the Breed's Origin

Because breeding records were secret, lost, or destroyed, there has been much speculation regarding the Weimaraner's ancestry. In the first half of the twentieth century, canine experts postulated various theories about the breeds used in the development of the Weimaraner. Although disproved, two theories in particular are often cited in the history of the Weimaraner.

Sometime after 1880, German connoisseurs of the Weimaraner first requested that the breed be recognized because of its excellent hunting qualities. However, many canine authorities strongly opposed the designation, because they believed that the Weimaraner was a color variation of the German Shorthair. However, in 1896, the Weimaraner was officially recognized as a distinct breed. Although the theory that the Weimaraner was a degenerated or faded color of the German Short-haired Pointer has often been revived over the years, the notion has been dismissed based on several criteria, including the fact that the Weimaraner is an older breed.

Another debunked theory contends that the Weimaraner was descended from the blue Great Dane, based on similarities in size, coat color and gloss, and shape of the head. However, this theory was discounted, because the blue Great Dane is a different color from the Weimaraner. Furthermore, the typical blue Great Dane has dark eyes, and the typical Weimaraner, including the blue, has light-colored eyes.

The Duke's Dog

The clearest and best-known history of the breed begins in central Germany in the early 1800s. The Grand Duke Karl August and the noblemen of the Court of Weimar used the Weimaraner to hunt large game. Big-game animals such as boar, wildcat, bear, and deer were abundant in the Thuringian Forest around Weimar. Athletic and powerful, the Weimaraner was an ideal dog to accompany the hunters. The dog's courage and protective instinct provided the perfect hunting combination when pursuing such formidable quarry as boar. Descended from hounds, the Weimaraners picked up their quarry's scent from the ground, ran the animal down, and then held it while baying until the huntsmen arrived.

With the encroachment of civilization, the wars and revolutions of 1848, and likely because hunters and their dogs were efficient, big game grew scarce. Consequently, the regular hunting of big game in Germany became rare. The hunters had to turn their attention to birds. The sportsmen nobles of Weimar began to develop the Weimaraner into a dog that could also hunt birds.

Hound dogs do not point. In order to change the breed from a trailing hound to a bird hunter, the Weimaraner was crossed with pointers. Of the several historic pointer breeds, it is thought that the Spanish Pointer, rather than the English Pointer, was the likely cross, giving the Weimaraner its size and light eye color.

The Weimaraner was developed primarily for the Duke, his family, high-ranking members of his court, and nobility. The Duke had great power and could dictate who could own the breed for hunting purposes. Until 1700, only the ruling classes in Germany were allowed to keep pointing dogs. The Duke continued this tradition. Carefully protected, the Weimaraner could not be owned as a pet.

A Protected Breed in Germany

The Weimaraner was developed to work in close association with people. While other hunting breeds were put in a kennel at the end of the day, the Weimaraner stayed at his master's side, sleeping and eating inside the home.

In the late nineteenth century, the Weimaraner was known as the king of hunting dogs. The breed's endurance, speed, courage, and exceptional tracking ability made it prized among sportsmen. Because he was a favorite of professional hunters and forest wardens, the Weimaraner was given the honorary title of "Forester's Dog." The Weimaraner was expected to be a versatile breed that could track, search, and indicate the location of various types of game, retrieve anything they could carry, show the handler the location of larger game, and protect the forester from attacking poachers.

Through the nineteenth century, the German upper class bred a limited number of Weimaraners under strict guidelines. When the German Weimaraner Club was established in 1897, one of the members' goals was to protect the breed rather than to promote it. The

A young Weimaraner in training for hunting.

nel. In 1951, the German Weimaraner Club was re-established in West Germany. The club reinstituted its original high standards and goals.

A Versatile Breed

The Weimaraner's keen nose and exceptional tracking abilities have led to its use in other fields besides hunting. In particular, the tracking achievements of two Weimaraners in the United States attracted attention during the late 1940s and early 1950s. Both dogs found lost people and convicts. The more famous dog located more than 60 people. Most noteworthy was his ability to make "finds" on cold trails that were several days old, trails on which even Bloodhounds had lost the scent. Such feats probably contributed to the Weimaraner's reputation as a wonder dog and fueled the breed's popularity during the 1950s. Weimaraners have also been used to track a variety of objects, including locating missile parts at the proving ground of the White Sands Missile Range during the early days of rocket testing.

club instituted rigid controls designed to retain the breed's superior qualifications as a hunter. A "breed and testing director" was responsible for assessing the dogs' conformation and coat quality. The dogs also had to pass a series of field-performance tests before they could be bred. Any dog who showed signs of weakness or poor qualities was not bred. The breed club was composed mainly of German aristocrats who were extremely selective in both club membership and placement of the dogs. Ownership of Weimaraners was restricted to individuals who could be trusted to follow the club's strict breeding practices.

Even with these breeding restrictions and selective membership, the Weimaraner spread to other European countries. However, both World Wars decimated the breed, and after World War I fewer than a dozen Weimaraners were reputed to have survived. After World War II, the breed's recovery in Europe was hindered during the American occupation. Regulations forbade hunting and possession of firearms except when accompanied by military person-

Today, in addition to competing in formal tracking tests, some owners and their Weimaraners are members of Search and Rescue canine units and assist in locating lost people. Although uncommon, Weimaraners have been used in bomb detection, as narcotics dogs, and for police work. In Germany, some owners qualify their dogs for Schutzhund degrees. In order to earn a Schutzhund title, a dog must pass a three-part test, which consists of tracking, obedience, and protection, all at the same trial.

In Germany, Weimaraners must typically qualify for breeding by meeting minimum requirements that include conformation and coat quality, genetic quality, and working ability. For these criteria, the dog must pass the spring and fall hunting examinations. Part of the hunting tests ensure that the breed's original protective dog qualities are retained by requiring that all Weimaraners demonstrate these protective instincts. Sometimes called "sharpness," this instinct is tested by experts in Schutzhund. The Weimaraner should demonstrate a self-confident protective impulse, but not viciousness. The dog should never attack without provocation. Because sharp dogs are potential liabilities, sharpness is not highly valued by American breeders.

The Weimaraner Arrives Stateside

While visiting and hunting in Germany, a Rhode Island advertising executive named Howard Knight was introduced to the Weimaraner by a friend. Mr. Knight became an enthusiastic admirer of the breed and wanted to acquire a pair to take back home to the United States. His friend sponsored his membership in the exclusive German Weimaraner Club, which was a prerequisite for ownership. Eventually Mr. Knight was approved for membership, but he had to take an oath to adhere to the rigorous German breeding protocols.

However, unknown to Mr. Knight and his friend, the first pair he received in 1929 were sterilized by radiation before they left Germany.

Weimaraner pups are born with blue eyes that change to amber as they mature.

Even though the pair could not be bred, they were good hunters. Knight was impressed with their ability to work a variety of birds, including ducks. They worked close to the hunter and were natural retrievers. It took nine more years, but Knight finally succeeded in importing three more Weimaraners. They reproduced and helped found the breed in North America.

The American Kennel Club (AKC) formally recognized the breed in 1942. The Weimaraner Club of America (WCA) was founded in 1943, and the first American breed standard was published the same year. After World War II, American servicemen returning to the United States brought home more Weimaraners. The

number of dogs imported from Germany remained quite high until the German Weimaraner Club began to function again in 1951. In addition to re-initiating a system to evaluate a dog's eligibility for breeding, the German club instituted a policy allowing only half of any litter to be sold to foreign buyers. By the end of the 1950s, few dogs were imported into the United States from Germany.

The 1950s Boom

In 1943, 32 Weimaraners were registered with the AKC. In 1950, slightly more than 1,000 were registered. By 1957, their numbers peaked with 10,011 new registrations. This population explosion was generated by tremendous publicity about the breed. In the late 1940s and early 1950s, the breed received enormously flattering coverage in newspapers and hunting magazines, helped along by the secretary of the Weimaraner Club of America, who acted as the breed's publicist. Stories of the Weimaraner's abilities, both real and phony, became known to the general public, as well as to hunters.

Besides exaggerated tales of the dog's hunting abilities, the press claimed the breed had the courage of a lion, the speed of a gazelle, the intellect of a genius, and the athletic abilities of a decathlon champion. The Weimaraner was sold as the breed that could do everything, including babysitting and answering the phone.

During this period, purebred dogs were highly regarded as status symbols. Given the Weimaraner's rarity, its history as a dog of German nobility, and its exotic appearance, Americans were enthralled with the breed. The demand was great for one of the dogs nicknamed the "Gray Ghost."

The dog graced numerous advertisements as a symbol of discriminating taste. Crowned with accolades such as superdog and wonderdog, the Weimaraner became a recognized status symbol. Celebrities such as Grace Kelly and political figures including President Eisenhower owned Weimaraners. Articles and photographs of these individuals with their Weimaraners kept the breed in the spotlight.

The Bane of Popularity

Striking good looks and mythical publicity had a cost. Naturally, the Weimaraner could not live up to the tall tales and wild claims. People concerned more with profit than with the integrity of the breed indiscriminately paired dogs and churned out puppies, which were sold at exorbitant prices. With little concern for the dogs' hunting abilities, temperament, or health, the quality of the breed declined. The breed that had been protected and carefully fostered in Germany became the victim of unscrupulous breeding.

In the 1960s, the exaggerated claims and poor breeding created a backlash. The Weimaraner lost popularity and was looked upon as a failure, especially among hunters. The number of new registrations declined, and in 1967, only 5,767 were registered.

Without the pressure of popularity, responsible breeders worked to correct the negative traits that had developed during the height of the breed's popularity. Through sound breeding practices, such as not breeding dogs with poor conformation or aggressive or shy temperaments, the Weimaraner became respectable again. Diligent breeders succeeded in restoring and preserving the breed's original qualities.

The Weimaraner Club of America

Like the German Weimaraner Club, which strives to protect and serve the breed rather than popularize it, the Weimaraner Club of America (for address, see page 92) adheres to similar goals. The WCA sponsors many activities and programs for its members, including a national specialty show and a national championship field trail. The club awards the titles Versatile Dog (V) and Versatile Dog Excellent (VX) to Weimaraners who have accumulated points in any three of six performance areas: show, hunting, retrieving, obedience, tracking, or agility. The monthly *Weimaraner Magazine* publishes information on current activities, show and field results, and articles on other topics, such as health concerns.

As a Hunter

The AKC classifies dogs into the following seven groups: sporting, hound, working, terrier, toy, non-sporting, and herding. The Weimaraner belongs to the Sporting Group. Other familiar breeds such as the Labrador and Golden Retriever also belong to this group. Unlike hounds, sporting breeds were not developed to chase and kill game.

Instead, these dogs were developed to help hunters with guns locate, flush, and retrieve game birds. Sporting dogs employ a variety of methods: Some, such as Pointers and Setters, point the location of the bird but do not flush it; some, such as Spaniels, flush the birds from their hiding places; and others, such as Labradors, wait in blinds with hunters to retrieve waterfowl. Sporting dogs have "soft mouths" as

they must bring the dead or injured bird to the hunter's hand without damaging the game.

The Weimaraner is used for hunting pheasant, quail, and other upland game birds, and waterfowl in good weather conditions. Known as a "gentleman's shooting dog," who searches the cover at a pace comfortable for a hunter on foot, Weimaraners are a close- to medium-ranging breed, which means that they are usually in the hunter's sight.

The Weimaraner has never caught on among North American hunters or recovered from its initial disastrous publicity blitz when it earned a reputation as a second-rate dog. Although many hunters have never hunted with a Weimaraner, they still have a poor opinion of the breed's abilities. However, the breed is beginning to emerge from this lingering prejudice.

The Weimaraner's hunting style is characterized by thoroughness of search rather than speed. Other sporting dogs, such as Pointers, are flashier, faster, and point with more style that often appeals more to hunters and field trial enthusiasts. The Weimaraner requires a softness or sensitivity on the trainer's part, which is different from the hard approach many gun dog owners are more familiar with.

The Weimaraner Standard

A breed standard is a written description of an individual breed. In addition to the physical characteristics, the breed standard includes such traits as temperament and gait. The standard portrays the ideal specimen; no dog will meet the standard in all respects. In a dog show, the winner is the individual that, in the judge's opinion, most closely meets the standard. The faults in each category of the breed standard help a judge evaluate an individual dog's good and bad qualities. The standard for the same breed can vary between countries. For example, the German standard accepts the longhaired Weimaraner, but the United States does not.

The breed standard is written by the breed's parent club, which is a national organization formed to supervise the breed's welfare. A standard can be amended over the years to meet the needs and desires of breeders. For example, the standard may change to permit or deny new colors. Any changes in the standard are initiated by a breed's parent club and must be approved by vote of the membership. The Weimaraner standard was modified six times since it was first adopted in 1943. The following is the current United States Weimaraner standard, which has been in effect since 1972.

General Appearance: A medium-sized gray dog with fine aristocratic features. He should present a picture of grace, speed, stamina, alertness, and balance. Above all, the dog's conformation must indicate the ability to work with great speed and endurance in the field.

Height: Height at the withers: dogs, 25 to 27 inches (62.5–67.5 cm); bitches, 23 to 25 inches (57.5–62.5 cm). One inch (2.5 cm) over or under the specified height of each sex is allowable but should be penalized. Dogs measuring less than 24 inches (60 cm) or more than 28 inches (70 cm) and bitches measuring less than 22 (5 cm) or more than 26 inches (65 cm) shall be disqualified.

This champion dog conforms closely to the breed standard.

The longhaired Weimaraner is uncommon (see page 15).

Temperament: The temperament should be friendly, fearless, alert, and obedient.

Very Serious Faults. Dogs exhibiting strong fear, shyness or extreme nervousness.

Gait: The gait should be effortless and should indicate smooth coordination. When seen from the rear, the hind feet should be parallel to the front feet. When viewed from the side, the topline should remain strong and level.

Major Fault. Poor gait.

Head and Neck: Moderately long and aristocratic, with moderate stop and slight median line extending back over the forehead. Rather prominent occipital bone and trumpets well set back, beginning at the back of the eye sockets. Measurement from tip of nose to stop equals that from stop to occipital bone. The flews should be straight, delicate at the nostrils. Skin drawn tightly. Neck clean-cut and moderately long. Expression kind, keen and intelligent.

Major Faults. Snipy muzzle. Neck too short, thick or throaty.

Ears: Long and lobular, slightly folded and set high. The ear when drawn snugly alongside the jaw should end approximately 2 inches (5 cm) from the point of the nose.

Major Fault. Short ears.

Eyes: In shades of light amber, gray or blue-gray, set well enough apart to indicate good disposition and intelligence. When dilated under excitement, the eyes may appear almost black.

The AKC standard for the Weimaraner.

Very Serious Fault. Eyes other than gray, blue-gray or light amber.

Teeth: Well set, strong and even; well developed and proportionate to jaw with correct scissors bite, the upper teeth protruding slightly over the lower teeth but not more than $\frac{1}{16}$ of an inch (.15 cm). Complete dentition is greatly desired.

Major Faults. Badly affected teeth. More than four teeth missing. Badly overshot, or undershot bite.

Nose: Gray.

Minor Fault. Pink Nose.

Lips and Gums: Pinkish flesh shades.

Very Serious Fault. Black mottled mouth.

Body: The body should be moderate in length, set in a straight line, strong, and should slope slightly from the withers. The chest should be well developed and deep with shoulders well laid back. Ribs well sprung and long. Abdomen firmly held; moderately tucked up flank. The brisket should extend to the elbow.

Major Faults. Back too long or too short. Faulty backs, either roached or sway.

Forelegs: Straight and strong, with measurement from the elbow to the ground approximately equaling the distance from the elbow to the top of the withers.

Major Faults. Elbows in or out. Feet east and west.

Hindquarters: Well-angulated stifles and straight hocks. Musculation well developed.

Major Fault. Cow-hocks.

Feet: Firm and compact, webbed, toes well arched, pads closed and thick, nails short and gray or amber in color.

Fault. Poor feet.

Dewclaws: Should be removed.

Tail: Docked. At maturity it should measure approximately 6 inches (15 cm) with a tendency to be light rather than heavy and should be carried in a manner expressing confidence and sound temperament. A non-docked tail shall be penalized.

Major Fault. Low-set tail. Very serious Fault. Non-docked tail.

Coat and Color: Short, smooth and sleek, solid color, in shades of mouse-gray to silver-gray, usually blending to lighter shades on the head and ears. A small white marking on the chest is permitted but should be penalized on any other portion of the body. White spots resulting from injury should not be penalized. A distinctly long coat is a disqualification. A distinctly blue or black coat is a disqualification.

Major Faults. Faulty coat. Very Serious Faults. White, other than a spot on the chest.

The Longhaired Weimaraner

The origin of this variety is unknown. The first longhaired Weimaraner was exhibited at a show in Germany in 1879. Longhaired Weimaraners are not that numerous in the United States, because they are not accepted in the WCA breed standard. They can compete in AKC obedience and field trials, but not in conformation shows or WCA events. The longhaired Weimaraner is recognized and shown in other countries, including Germany. Repeated attempts by some United States club members to gain formal recognition of the longhaired Weimaraner have failed over the years.

Long hair is a recessive trait carried by some shorthaired Weimaraners. Longhaired Weimaraners born in a litter from shorthaired parents indicates that one of the parents carries the trait. The tails of longhaired dogs are not docked. Occasionally, because the long coat can be difficult to detect when the puppies are only a few days old, a longhaired's tail is docked. Only the last two vertebrae are removed if the tail is intentionally docked. The longhaired Weimaraner is the antithesis of the breed's sleek, muscled look. Unlike the breed's wash-and-wear short coat, the hairs between a longhaired's toes can knot, track mud, and also collect ice in bad weather.

The German standard also describes one other coat type called *Stockhaarig,* associated with offspring from a shorthaired and longhaired breeding. Somewhat between two coat types, it is rare in Germany and not mentioned in any other Weimaraner standard.

The Illegal Blue

Sometimes advertised as "rare blue," this color is not accepted in the United States breed standard. The blue Weimaraner has a controversial history because of suspicions that the original progenitor of the blue Weimaraner, Cäsar von Gaiberg, was crossbred. Cäsar was imported from a reputable breeder in Germany to the United States in 1949. Because of his unusual color and dark nose, along with a qualification on his German papers, many questioned his breeding. Cäsar was accepted and registered by the AKC; therefore all his offspring are also eligible for registration. Nonetheless, the blue controversy, as it came to be called, grew more heated. Eventually, the WCA membership voted to disqualify blues in the 1971 standard.

While the normal Weimaraner coat color is varying shades of gray, all colors have a brown undertone. The blue Weimaraner's coat has a black undertone.

The blue color is dominant over the silver gray color. One or both parents must be blue for blue puppies to appear in a litter. Many people find the blue Weimaraner attractive. As with the longhaired variety, attempts to have the blue color recognized in the breed standard have failed.

UNDERSTANDING YOUR WEIMARANER

About Purebred Dogs

For thousands of years, people have used selective breeding to retain specific desirable traits in dogs. Through selective breeding, people developed dog breeds that varied from one another in size, shape, color, temperament, and behavioral characteristics, such as swimming well.

In addition to a uniform and recognizable physique and color, each breed has a unique set of characteristics and personality traits. Knowing a dog's breed is a good way to predict its activity level, intelligence, and personality. Although some breeds, such as those in the Toy Group, were developed just for companionship, most breeds were developed for specific jobs, such as herding sheep, helping huntsmen, killing vermin, and guarding livestock. Some breeds, such as hounds, were developed to work independently of people, and are aloof, barely willing to acknowledge that people exist. Other breeds, such as the Weimaraner, were bred to work in close association with people.

Because there is a genetic component to temperament, behavior, and working ability, many breeds almost automatically do the work for which they were bred. For example, Border Collies herd their families if they have no live-

Originally, Weimaraners were bred to be energetic dogs that could work in the fields all day.

stock to herd. Retrievers fetch balls and sticks if their owner does not hunt. These aspects of a dog's behavior are transmitted from generation to generation through inheritance. Because purebreds are developed through generations of selective breeding, the selected traits still show up.

The AKC recognizes more than 150 dog breeds. However, the original purpose for the development of many breeds might be at odds with modern life, such as dogs bred specifically to fight other dogs or other animals—the Bull Mastiff, for example. People still keep and enjoy such breeds, but they might require special consideration. In other cases, some breeds became extinct when the original purpose for which they were bred was no longer necessary.

People are attracted to purebred dogs for a variety of reasons, including their looks, size, behavior, and temperament. Dog breeds can go in and out of fashion depending on their star status. Movies depicting particular breeds, such as Disney's *101 Dalmatians*, often spur a burst in a breed's popularity.

Like many breeds in the sporting group, Weimaraners were bred to be energetic dogs that could work in the field all day. The traits selected over generations strongly affect the modern Weimaraner. Even when not used for their original purpose, Weimaraners retain their energetic character.

Is the Weimaraner the Right Dog for You?

People are attracted to Weimaraners for a variety of reasons, but many are drawn to the breed's classy appearance. The Weimaraner is a beautiful dog with a glossy, unique coat color and eyes of startling hues.

Many people who surrender their dogs to Weimaraner Rescue state: "Nobody told me they needed this much—(pick one or more) time, attention, exercise—oh, but they're so pretty." Beyond the Weimaraner's striking good looks is a reality of what it is like to live with this particular breed. Some things are best admired from afar; the Weimaraner might be one of those.

Realistically assessing the breed's traits, together with your lifestyle and expectations, can help you determine whether a Weimaraner is right for you. The Weimaraner has been described as a breed that you love or hate. What is perfect for one person might be perfectly awful for another.

Generalizations about the nature of a dog breed can be complicated and fraught with contradictions. There are always some fanciers who will vehemently disagree with a statement or those who will point out exceptions. Nonetheless, generalizations are useful to give a potential owner an idea of what a particular breed of dog might be like, although, naturally, much depends on other factors, such as the dog's home environment.

Weimaraner ownership requires three factors:
✔ They must be a part of your family life.
✔ They need vigorous daily exercise.
✔ They need obedience training.

These are not areas you can neglect and expect to have a rewarding relationship with your Weimaraner. In fact, with such neglect, you and your Weimaraner might just be miserable.

Part of the Family

The Weimaraner is a good choice for someone who truly wants a canine companion integrated into his or her life. Weimaraners require daily attention and human companionship. They like people and want to be with their owners constantly. A Weimaraner will follow you from room to room, even shoving open the bathroom door. When you sit on the couch, chances are your Weimaraner will be lying down so that he is touching you. Weimaraners will want to be involved in everything that is going on and go everywhere you go. They love riding in the car and visiting other people. Some people find such behavior charming and endearing, while others might be driven crazy by it.

The Weimaraner was developed to share his master's home and hearth, and the breed retains this desire. This dog will not lie in a corner and wait for you to be ready. If isolated or neglected in a kennel or backyard, with only occasional attention, a Weimaraner will become hyperactive, destructive, and neurotic.

These behavioral characteristics do not mean that a Weimaraner cannot belong to a single person. However, someone who is gone at work all day and goes out most nights will soon have a wretched, destructive dog at home. The Weimaraner must be part of your life, and not just on weekends.

Exercise

Weimaraners need vigorous exercise every day. A walk around one or two blocks on a leash at the end of a work or school day might not suffice. The breed has a high activity level and needs to run. The Weimaraner is a good choice for someone who is active and likes to bike, jog, or hike, and anticipates such activities continuing for the next ten years (the dog's projected active life span). Games of fetch and swimming are other forms of exercise that a Weimaraner will enjoy.

Bred to go all day, the Weimaraner can run some people ragged. When you come home tired from work, your Weimaraner will greet you at the door, ready to play. A Weimaraner can go on a long run in the morning, collapse and snooze for several hours and be ready to go again a few hours later.

A fenced yard is necessary. However, the yard is not a substitute for interactive exercise with you. Few dogs will run and play by themselves; they usually wait for their owner. Some Weimaraners can adapt to apartment living, as long as they are provided with *numerous* outings each day.

Many people interested in the Weimaraner want to know whether they are hyperactive. The answer depends on your lifestyle. The breed is energetic and fits in well with active people. However, those used to a sedate, short-legged breed might find the Weimaraner too energetic. A properly trained and socialized Weimaraner is not so wound up that he cannot focus. But beware that without adequate exercise, a Weimaraner will seem high-strung.

A Weimaraner deprived of sufficient exercise might become destructive, not out of spite, but because the dog is bored and needs something to do. A bored Weimaraner will look for amusement. He might dig up the backyard, bark excessively, dig the stuffing out of a sofa,

or try to escape from home or yard. Such activities are more interesting to this intelligent breed than lounging around all day waiting for you to come home.

Obedience Training

The Weimaraner needs basic obedience training. When trained and properly socialized, a Weimaraner can be a wonderful family pet. However, a puppy will not grow into a secure, well-behaved adult without patience and proper training. Expect to spend the first year working with your Weimaraner. This groundwork is essential. Lack of structured training can lead to problems.

Weimaraners are a slow-maturing breed. Puppyhood can last a long time, sometimes between two and three years. When they are past their wild and woolly puppy stage, Weimaraners settle down and are great dogs. However, with some individual dogs, this might not be for four years.

As a breed, Weimaraners are affectionate and have a strong desire to please, but some have a stubborn streak. Obstinate individual dogs know you cannot correct them when they are off leash and you are far away. Such dogs can be more challenging to train. However, Weimaraners are also sensitive, and severe training methods can ruin their trust.

The Weimaraner is an intelligent dog that responds best to clear rules. Weimaraner owners must have the personal fortitude to provide a disciplined framework early on and throughout their dog's life. Because they can take advantage of novices, the Weimaraner is not necessarily the best choice for a first-time dog owner. If the dog does not think you mean a given command or you are not tough enough to ensure compliance, it can cause frustration and problems.

Other Traits

How easy training will be can be defined by the dog's desire to please, willingness to comply, and responsiveness to commands. Weimaraners are rated as average to high on this scale. Like all dogs, Weimaraners learn some commands right away, while other commands take more time. As long as a command is clearly communicated, many Weimaraners learn quickly, which is very rewarding. Even when they do not understand a command, they often come up with an innovative response in their strong desire to please. However, some individual dogs exercise their own discretion when it comes to obeying certain commands they clearly understand and when deciding whether they should obey a command the first or second time it is given. They are a clever breed and try to communicate their needs to their owners, to the point that many train their owners to play various games with them, such as hide-and-seek.

Weimaraners are considered average to exceptional in problem-solving aptitude, which is a good measurement of canine intelligence. Many owners discover that their dogs are mischievous and curious. An oft-repeated refrain among Weimaraner owners is that their dogs think they are people. A predilection for opening various types of cabinets and helping themselves to edible contents might contribute to this statement. Owners must sometimes resort to putting childproof latches on cupboards. While they do not all demonstrate this proclivity, many Weimaraners are also capable of opening doors. Some individuals are not above sneaking food off countertops or licking dirty dishes sitting in the sink. Naturally, dogs with such tendencies can be challenging to live with and must be thwarted and taught their place.

Weimaraners are observant and have a tendency to copy the actions of other dogs. This behavior can be useful when a puppy copies the behavior of an obedient older dog. By watching the older dog, a puppy can quickly learn to sit for a treat or to follow the dog out

Weimaraners like to snuggle!

Weimaraners are a very intelligent breed, but they need formal training.

a dog door. This copycat behavior is amusing when the puppy mimics the habits of other breeds. Thus, a Weimaraner puppy who grows up with a Chesapeake Bay Retriever might also try to dive for rocks under water. The drawback is that a Weimaraner puppy will copy both the good and bad habits of the older dog.

Protectiveness

Weimaraners are different from other sporting breeds because they have a more highly developed protective instinct. This trait was valued and cultivated by the breed's developers in Germany; they wanted a dog that could protect his master from poachers and dangerous big game animals such as wild boar.

This protective trait should be exhibited only under appropriate circumstances. Typically, adult Weimaraners will bark to alert their owners to the presence of strangers, other dogs, or disruptions such as delivery trucks. Some are more protective and growl menacingly when a stranger approaches the home or their owners, but should stop when told. However, even a protective dog should never exhibit viciousness, which is a highly undesirable trait and is considered a serious fault.

Some breeds tend to be possessive of objects including their food dish and toys. Weimaraners do not exhibit this tendency. Nonetheless, they should be taught to relinquish objects when asked and to not display guarding behavior.

Creatures of Comfort

For all their rugged athletic abilities, Weimaraners are creatures of comfort and seek the most comfortable places to repose. This might be a toasty spot with the cat in front of the fireplace, or part way over your lap on the couch. They will readily sit on chairs at the dining table and sleep on couches and beds. You must decide early on what furniture, if any, you will share with your Weimaraner.

Many Weimaraners do share their owners' beds, comfortably snoozing with their heads on the pillows. Because a Weimaraner's coat is short and sleek, the bed stays relatively clean of hair and dirt. A *New York Times* reporter interviewing William Wegman about his famous Weimaraners, noted how free of hair the white coverlet on the master bed was, inasmuch as the reporter knew the dogs shared the bed. Mr. Wegman responded simply, "Oh, they sleep under the covers." Indeed, this is a common scenario with which many owners are familiar. Such people note that their dogs are good at cuddling and prefer to crawl under the covers on especially cold nights.

When picking up a puppy, be sure to support the hindquarters.

Male or Female?

The choice of gender usually has to do with personal preference. Choose the gender for which you feel more of an affinity. A person's preference for one sex over the other is often based on previous personal experience and/or anecdote. There are no documented differences between the sexes for obedience, problem-solving ability, or affection.

Both sexes are loving and loyal, and any differences between them do not affect those traits. Like many breeds, the male Weimaraner is, on average, both taller and heavier than the female—70 to 85 pounds (31.5–38 kg) compared to 55 to 65 pounds (25–29 kg), on average. Besides being physically larger and stronger, some males are more vigorous in activity. Some more subtle differences might include a slightly blockier head and stockier build for the male; females are often more slender and delicate looking. However, these are generalizations that might not always apply, depending on the dogs' breeding.

The most significant personality differences between the sexes are apparent in dogs that are not neutered or spayed. Intact males can be more difficult to control and command. If not kept in a fenced area, they are more likely to roam. They can also become dominant and aggressive toward other males, more likely to fight with other male dogs, and may become overly protective of their home and people. These traits do not usually appear until the male is at least two years old. (Early castration eliminates these behavioral difficulties and neutered males generally have a longer life span than intact males.)

Intact males lift their leg to urinate and mark their territory. Hence, the trees and bushes in your yard will be marked, and it can take longer to walk a male around the block since he will want to stop and mark every few yards. Some fixed males tend to urinate all at once, or to mark significantly less.

Some breeders say the intact female is manipulative; she can be sweet when she feels like it, or aloof when she is not in the mood for attention. Twice a year, an unspayed female will come into season for several weeks. Females in season can be messy and sometimes moody. During this time, a female is receptive to intact males and can become pregnant. Free-roaming, unneutered dogs—or dogs that get loose (and they will get loose) because of her alluring aroma—will congregate at your home to try to mate with the female. They can be a noisy, brawling bunch.

More than One Puppy?

No, do not buy more than one puppy! In particular, couples should resist the temptation to get "his and her" puppies. Many Weimaraners given to breed rescue come from homes where two puppies were acquired at the same time. There are many reasons it is difficult to have two puppies at the same time. Two puppies will bond with each other, not with you. It can be hard to find enough time to spend alone with one puppy, let alone spend individual time with two. Two puppies will get into twice as much trouble as one. Difficulties arise when you must discipline one puppy without the other's wincing, because he thinks you are also scolding him. Two puppies will be twice as hard to train as one. And if a mess is made in the house, you will not know which puppy needs more help with housebreaking.

Other more complex problems can arise with two puppies. For example, different dogs have different temperaments. One may respond rapidly to training, while the other requires much more work to learn the same behaviors. Finally, keep in mind that dogs of the same age are more likely to die around the same time. It is difficult for an owner to lose two dogs around the same time, but it is also difficult for the dog that loses his best friend.

If you are concerned about your puppy having a playmate, especially when grown, it is far more sensible to arrange play sessions with a neighbor's or friend's dog. It can work out quite well for the two dogs, who often become good friends. Arrangements can be made to alternate at whose home the dogs will play.

After your first puppy is grown, well socialized, and obedience trained (about two years old), then you can consider adding another dog.

Children

In general, Weimaraners are good family dogs that enjoy having people around. They love children and enjoy attention. However, like any dog, a Weimaraner who has never met children is less likely to exhibit such tendencies. Because Weimaraners are a large, strong breed, they must be taught to properly interact with a variety of people, including children (see Socialization on page 55).

Other Pets

If properly introduced while still a puppy, many Weimaraners accept and even become "friends" with other household dogs. However, experiences vary with other small pets like cats and rabbits. Because they were bred to hunt small and large game, some Weimaraners might be inclined to chase or attack another pet. Although introductions work best when your dog is still a puppy, many adult dogs can be trained to accept another animal as part of the family. Supervise any introduction and all initial interactions. Make sure the animals are fine with one another before you leave them alone together.

Lifespan

The lifespan of Weimaraners ranges from about ten to twelve years, although some live up to fifteen years. Weimaraners are a slow maturing breed and do not reach their full size until they are about two years old. While their maximum height is reached by one year of age, they continue to fill out for another year.

SELECTING A WEIMARANER

Should You Own a Dog?

Whether purebreed or mixed, all dogs require time and energy. Some independent breeds might require less of your time, but the Weimaraner is a breed that requires a lot of time and companionship. Dogs are completely dependent on people; if you do not have enough time, a better choice for a pet might be the more independent cat. Caring for a dog should be fun, not a chore. Owning a dog is a huge responsibility that is often easier to share with family or housemates. Modern life is so busy that many people do not have time for a dog. Dogs can also be expensive. Besides the initial purchase price of your Weimaraner, there are food costs and veterinary expenses, both expected and unexpected.

The Modern Dog

Surveys in the last decade indicate that Americans are working more hours than ever before. Many behavioral problems in Weimaraners occur because the dogs are left alone all day and find destructive ways to amuse themselves.

Be patient at first—your puppy may be frightened when you first bring him home.

Many pet services are available that can make owning a dog easier for working people, especially if you have extra money to budget for your dog's care. *Dog walkers* and *dog day care* are two of the best options for working Weimaraner owners. Businesses such as dog walkers and dog day care are more common in large urban areas than in rural areas.

While such services might strike some people as frivolous, the Weimaraner was not developed to sit in a fenced backyard with minimal human contact and exercise. Proper care of your Weimaraner entails providing for his needs. Using such businesses will not make your dog any less devoted to you but can actually make your canine companion healthier and more pleasurable to be around. When you come home from work, your Weimaraner is less likely to leap at you like a warrior if he has had some exercise earlier in the day. A Weimaraner that goes eagerly with his walker or to his day care indicates he is well-trained and socialized.

These businesses can be found through your veterinarian, pet stores, and phone book. A day care facility should be clean, have a schedule of activities, and knowledgeable staff. Be sure to visit the facility and check references before leaving your dog. These services can be expensive, but using them two to three times a week is often sufficient for your dog.

Even if such businesses are not available where you live, a resourceful Weimaraner owner can find other options. A trustworthy friend or neighbor who loves dogs, but does not own one, might be interested in taking your dog on a jog, walk, or hike. The only drawbacks are that the friend must know how to handle the dog and such exercise might not be as regular as a paid service. (Children younger than mid-teens are often physically less capable of handling a large, powerful Weimaraner.)

Dog play groups are often informal associations of dog owners who meet to let their dogs play off leash in areas such as dog parks or other locations where dogs are allowed to run freely. The owners can visit while their dogs run and play. A well-socialized Weimaraner can expend his energy in a fun, nondestructive manner.

Some people whose dogs are "good friends" arrange to drop one dog off at the other's home, so the dogs can play together during the day. However, be careful about leaving any toys or bones that could spark a confrontation. It should be noted that in some cases, just like young children, dogs do not play as enthusiastically unless they have an audience.

Some businesses allow employees to bring their well-behaved dogs to work. The companies often have formal policies, which require the dog to be licensed, have current vaccinations, and be well trained. Office dogs are known to reduce employee stress and naturally, the dogs also benefit. Of course, if your home is your workplace, your dog also can benefit.

Other Considerations

Bringing home a new puppy is exciting, but it also means a commitment of time and energy. Any puppy takes time, especially the first few weeks when you and your puppy are establishing a routine. Plan to acquire your puppy when you will have the maximum amount of time available for his care. For many people, this is during the summer, a weekend, or a holiday (often excluding the hectic Christmas season). The least desirable times to bring home a new puppy include moving to a new home, a new job, a job promotion that might require your absence for travel or more time away from home, or when expecting a baby.

Expect to make a large commitment of time the first year of your Weimaraner puppy's life. During the first year, you will house-train him, take him to obedience classes, and socialize him so he is used to a variety of people and places. The initial training requires great effort but has tremendous rewards; you are developing the foundation for a companion who will share your life for the next 10 to 15 years. Your investment in time can prevent the development of undesirable habits in your Weimaraner.

In some parts of the country, the time of year might affect your decision on when to acquire your puppy. Housebreaking a puppy in cold, snowy weather can be difficult. Both you and your puppy are likely to be miserable if the outside temperatures are freezing. Going outside can be especially unpleasant if you need to leave your warm bed to take the puppy outside in the middle of the night (Your puppy will not like going outside anymore than you will.). In such cold regions, the best time to acquire a puppy might be anytime but winter.

Where to Buy Your Weimaraner

Before you buy, you should know why you want a Weimaraner: pet, show, field, or personal gun dog. This knowledge will help you focus your search for the best possible breeders. The Weimaraner Club of America (address on page 92) can provide lists of breeders in your area.

Reputable Breeders

Serious breeders who show their dogs, compete in field trials or obedience competitions, or regularly hunt with their dogs, usually have waiting lists for puppies. Individuals on the waiting list eagerly await certain breedings, because the puppies will be more likely to have the qualities in which they are interested. In many cases, all the puppies from a given breeding are already sold before they are even whelped.

Reputable breeders know the Weimaraner. They will have spent time and money proving that the sire and dam are physically and mentally sound, and fit the breed standard. Their dogs might have points or championship titles in shows or field trials. To produce the best possible puppies, they will match pedigrees and abilities.

Knowledgeable breeders will have their dogs' hips x-rayed and rated by the Orthopedic Foundation for Animals (OFA). Doing so will reduce the incidence of hip dysplasia. This process cannot typically be done until the dog is two years old; thus, the dam and sire should be at least two years of age. Knowledgeable breeders often check for other potential hereditary diseases in Weimaraners, such as thyroid disease.

The puppies are raised in a warm, clean environment, then properly socialized so they do not have preventable temperament problems. Rep-utable breeders will ask you questions to make sure the breed will fit into your life. They are available to answer any questions you might have about your dog. If you cannot keep your dog at any time during his life, the breeder will often take back the dog and find him a new home. Furthermore, such breeders are interested in and will keep track of any hereditary problems that result from specific pairings.

Backyard Breeders

"Backyard breeder" is a derogatory term referring to someone who puts a pair of dogs of the same breed together, without researching the dogs' backgrounds. Such breeders can be unscrupulous and interested in money more than in the welfare of the puppies or breed. There are exceptions, however, and some can breed satisfactory dogs.

Puppies advertised in the classified section of newspapers are typically from backyard breeders. One can often obtain a reasonable pet-quality dog from such a source. However, the newspaper is not necessarily the place to look for a show or field-quality puppy. Be wary of putting too much value on the statement "champion bloodlines." This usually means a couple of champions might be in the puppies' pedigree, but they are often four or five generations ago. At the very least, inquire whether the sire and dam have been certified by the Orthopedic Foundation for Animals for hips rated at least "good."

Pet Stores

The least desirable place to obtain a Weimaraner puppy is from a pet store. Puppies from pet stores can be more difficult to housebreak because they have urinated and defecated in their den-like enclosures. More significantly, the puppies have missed important socialization and have not been kept as part of a family environment, either with people or other canines. Puppies from pet stores are more likely to develop separation anxiety, because they were isolated during a critical period in their social development. Because the puppies might have been weaned from their mother too soon, they might not know how to inhibit the strength of their bite—something it is much easier for a mother dog and siblings to teach than for a human.

How Old?

Weimaraner puppies are born with zebra stripes that fade after about three days. When the puppies are three days old, their tails are docked and their dewclaws are removed. The best age to acquire your Weimaraner puppy is between seven and eight weeks of age. By seven weeks of age, puppies begin to take an active interest in playing and interacting with people. The puppy will bond with humans between the ages of seven and twelve weeks of age.

By eight weeks the puppy is ready to learn and needs human company and stimulation.

If you are buying your puppy long-distance, be aware that most airlines will not allow puppies to fly until they are at least eight weeks of age.

Types

Show or Pet Quality

You might find that a breeder has rated some puppies show quality and others as pet quality. Based on years of experience, a breeder can make an educated guess about a puppy's show potential. However, no breeder can guarantee such things. The breeder can point out certain features of a show-quality puppy when compared to the littermates who are rated pet quality. Besides soundness of construction and balance (how the puppy is put together), some

Breeders chart the growth and development of their puppies.

By eight weeks of age, your pup should be ready and willing to learn.

Be sure to supervise children and puppies for the safety of both.

puppies stand out with a confident disposition. If you plan to show your Weimaraner, you should familiarize yourself with the Breed Standard.

A pet quality puppy has features that would make it difficult to successfully compete in conformation shows, such as a short neck, but these show ring faults do not affect the puppy's ability to function. Likewise, too much white on the chest or elsewhere on the body will not affect the puppy's ability to live a long happy life as a pet. During his first scheduled visit, your veterinarian should be able to detect any serious structural problems that could adversely affect your puppy.

Personal Gun Dog and/or Field Trial

There is a history of disdain among hunters toward their breed's show dog brethren. In many hunters' opinions, numerous gun dog breeds, including the Irish Setter, Cocker Spaniel, and Weimaraner have been ruined for their original purposes by the pet and show stock. Show breeders select and exaggerate certain attractive traits that make the dog less practical in the field. Traits that catch a judge's eye, such as larger size or long flowing coats, are different from those needed by a hunter. Even worse, show dog lines have had the "hunt" or working ability bred out of them.

These breeds, including the Weimaraner, have split into two different types: one for fieldwork and one for show. However, many serious breeders work to retain the breed's hunting instincts and preserve the Weimaraner as one breed, both showing and hunting their dogs.

Nonetheless, a hunter who wants a Weimaraner for a personal gun dog is best advised to contact breeders who have field lines and who compete in field trials, or to contact the North American Versatile Hunting Dog Association (NAVHDA) (see page 92) for a list of breeders. Through NAVHDA, whose members focus on producing dogs for hunters, you can locate Weimaraner breeders who might have hunting line puppies available.

Field trial dogs are high-performance athletes that need to be able to compete at the highest physical and mental level. Compared to other versatile dog breeds, relatively few Weimaraners compete in field trials. To find a Weimaraner with good field trial potential, contact breeders who compete in these events, the Weimaraner Club of America for help locating breeders of field dogs, or the AKC for a list of hunt and retrieve clubs in your area (for addresses see page 92).

Important Papers

When you buy your puppy, the breeder will give you a copy of the puppy's pedigree, registration application, health record, and sometimes a sales contract. The pedigree is a chronological list of your puppy's ancestors for three or more generations. It will show the ancestors' registered names and indicate whether they earned any show, field, or obedience titles. Titles in recent generations are more meaningful than those several generations back. The registration application transfers ownership of the puppy to you from the breeder. To register your puppy, you must mail the form to the AKC. The health record contains a list of the inoculations the puppy has received and when the vaccines were given. It should also indicate when and with what your puppy was wormed. The record will also specify whether your puppy had any other veterinary treatment. Some breeders also use a sales contract that guarantees the puppy's health and temperament and specifies certain conditions with which you must comply, such as following a specific vaccination schedule and spaying or neutering.

Price

A Weimaraner is not inexpensive, although they vary in price depending on where you live. Generally, they cost more in urban areas, especially along the east and west coasts. Although they are less expensive in rural areas, either way expect to spend more than several hundred dollars. Show quality puppies or those from champion parents (show or field) will cost even more.

What to Look for in a Healthy Weimaraner

Once you are at a breeder's home or kennel, look to make sure the premises are odor-free and clean. You should always be able to see the mother, called the "dam." However, often the male, called the "sire," is not present. The breeder researched and selected the best mate for the dam, and in many cases, the male dog belongs to someone else and lives elsewhere, even across the country. However, the breeder will have photographs and information on the sire, such as his shoulder height, weight, and whether he has any titles or points toward a championship.

A healthy puppy will feel solid and have a clean glossy coat. He should not feel frail and bony, or have a bloated belly. Make sure the puppies have clean eyes and noses, with no discharge from the ears. The best health insurance is to make sure the sale terms include your veterinarian's examination of the puppy.

The puppies in a litter of Weimaraners can look alike. How can you decide which one is right for you? Most likely the breeder will help you in this decision by asking questions. Conscientious breeders are interested in making the best possible match for each puppy and new owner. They have watched the puppies for seven or eight weeks and know each puppy's character and personality. Listen to the breeder's recommendations. The breeder will know which puppy is best suited to a family where it can enjoy a quiet life and creature comforts, and which puppies are more inquisitive and outgoing and better suited for boisterous families. In some cases, a breeder might have performed puppy personality tests. Such tests can be helpful in identifying individuals that are aggressive and dominant from those that are timid and passive. Trust your instincts and do not rush to buy a puppy. You are choosing a companion who will share your home for the next decade.

For many people, playing with a litter of puppies is a delightful aspect of selecting their new puppy. But this is not necessarily the best way to choose your puppy. The tendency is to pick the forceful puppy that shoves his way ahead of the others to visit with you. Such an individual is likely to be the dominant one in the litter and the toughest to train. Do not buy more dog than you need. A bold puppy might seem attractive but will require more effort and time to keep occupied. If your Weimaraner will be a family pet, get the family sedan model, not the Formula One racing model, which is more suited to a life competing in field trials.

Consider an Adult Dog

Few people purchase a puppy with the expectation that they will later have to get rid of him. However, every year thousands of animals become homeless. Weimaraners need new homes for the same reasons as other breeds, including divorce, death, a family move, and not enough time. Older puppies and adult dogs are available for adoption through local and national Weimaraner rescue groups. The national organization's address is listed on page 92 and local groups' addresses are available through the national organization's Internet site.

While obtaining a grown dog means you might bypass difficult puppy stages such as housebreaking, older dogs are not always free of problems. Adult dogs can be more set in their ways and some might have bothersome habits such as begging or barking. A disobedient puppy can also be easier to contend with than a grown dog. Rescue groups typically screen dogs for health problems and temperament before placing them for adoption. They know the dogs' personalities and peccadilloes and work to make the best fit between an adopter and dog.

CARE OF THE WEIMARANER PUPPY

As he snuggles in your arms for security, it is exciting to carry a lovable Weimaraner puppy into your house for the first time. His beautiful blue eyes, huge "dumbo" ears, large paws, and silky oversized suit of fur carry the promise of unlimited potential. As your puppy tentatively licks your hand, you can dream of future adventures. However, a lot of work is ahead, much of it enjoyable if approached correctly. But before you even get your puppy through the door, you can ensure a happy existence by preparing for him and incorporating him into your daily routine.

Equipment

Before you bring home your puppy, you should purchase the following items:

✔ crate
✔ bed
✔ collar
✔ leash
✔ identification tag
✔ food
✔ water bowls
✔ toys

Caring for a new puppy is a family affair.

Crate

A crate should be considered essential. Some pet owners, especially first-time owners, are reluctant to use a crate because they think it is a cruel cage. However, not only will a crate help you keep your sanity, but your puppy will see the crate as his own private bedroom or den and a safe place in which to retreat. Crate training is also advantageous if your dog ever needs to travel by air, since he will already be used to a crate.

Although yet another expense, a crate is one of the best investments you can make. A crate is invaluable in house-training, which is discussed in detail on page 42. Two types of crates are available: rigid plastic crates with ventilation holes and wire doors, which are approved by airlines for shipping animals, or heavy-gauge wire-frame crates, which are often collapsible for easy storage. Either type will suffice, although the plastic crate provides a cozier den so the puppy is not as easily disturbed by household activities. A blanket draped over a wire crate will serve the same purpose.

You can buy a small crate that will suit your puppy for several months, or you can purchase one that is suitable for your puppy's adult size. Although dogs are den animals and generally do not eliminate in their dens or sleeping areas, puppies may soil at the end of the crate farthest from their sleeping area if the crate is too large. If you buy an adult-sized crate, you might need to temporarily reduce the crate's size by blocking off a portion with a piece of plywood.

When your puppy is ready for a nap, you can put him to sleep in his crate and close the door. When he is ready to wake up and come out, he will whimper. The crate will give you peace of mind and freedom to pursue other activities while your puppy is sleeping. When your puppy wakes up from a nap, he cannot void while he finds you, nor can he grab and destroy various items lying about. Fewer accidents and occasions to correct your puppy reduce stress for both of you.

Many puppies readily enter and use their crate. If necessary, encourage your puppy to use his crate by placing toys or food treats at the back of the crate. Do put a crate mat or an inexpensive blanket inside. When some puppies teethe, they might chew the bedding. Ripped and shredded bedding will still provide a comfortable nest for the puppy. However, he could accidentally swallow a piece of bedding, which might cause a digestive blockage. Providing him with an alternative chew toy inside his crate, such as a hard bone, can help prevent this potential problem. Otherwise, you might need to remove the bedding.

While a crate is a valuable tool, there are times it should not be used. The crate is a safe refuge, not a prison or a place of punishment. Do not leave your puppy unattended in his crate for more than a few hours. Older puppies between three to four months of age should not be left for more than three to four hours. Do not lock your puppy in his crate when he is boisterous and needs to run and play. If you are away from home all day, you will not be able to leave your puppy in his crate, unless someone is available to *regularly* take the puppy outside every few hours and to also play with him. If you need a few moments of free time, you may put your puppy in his crate as long as you provide him with a suitable chew toy or other item with which to play.

You must decide right away whether you will use a crate for your puppy. An older, adolescent puppy is less likely to accept a crate as his den and will have a fit if you try to suddenly confine him in a crate.

Bed

Provide your puppy with a comfortable bed or a nest of blankets in which he can rest, sleep, and chew his toys. The bed can be in addition to his crate, or it can fit inside his crate. Either way, choose a bed with a removable cover so that it, like the blankets, can be easily washed. Puppies are playful and have no concept of how much their bed might have cost. Some puppies might decide to stalk, attack, and destroy their bed. If your puppy shows such propensities, wait to get the designer bed that coordinates with your house until your puppy is grown.

Collar

Purchase a flat buckle collar for your puppy. Your puppy might initially scratch at his collar, but he will soon get used to it. A puppy will outgrow several collars before he has finished growing. Some economical collars are designed to expand as your puppy grows and can last for many months before a new one is needed. For proper fit, two fingers should readily fit between the collar and your puppy's neck. A collar is necessary to attach your puppy's identification and leash. Do not use a choke collar for these purposes. The choke collar is a training tool and in most cases you will not need one for your Weimaraner puppy until he is about six months old.

Identification

Immediately attach an identification tag with your address and telephone number to your puppy's collar. A variety of identification tags are available, ranging from metal and plastic ones that are ordered through the mail to temporary identification such as small tubes in which the owner's name and address are written on paper. Because identification tags can accidentally fall off, it is prudent to write your phone number in permanent marker directly on your puppy's collar.

More sophisticated methods of identification include inserting a microchip the size of a grain of rice under the dog's skin at the base of the neck, and tattooing. Many veterinary hospitals and shelter facilities have scanners for the microchips, which can identify the dog and the owner's relevant information. A tattoo is usually done on the inside of a dog's thigh. You can have your dog tattooed with your social security number, AKC number, driver's license number, or even phone number. The first two numbers are the most reliable, especially if you ever move to another state. If you use your social security number, for a small fee you can register your dog with the National Registry. Because the microchip and tattoo are not readily interpreted by a stranger who finds your dog, an identification tag affixed to your dog's

You'll soon learn that a pooper scooper is really man's best friend.

collar is still recommended. Your veterinarian, local Weimaraner club, or humane society can help you locate relevant services in your area.

Leash

Most basic obedience classes require a 6-foot (180 cm) leash, not a 4-foot (120 cm) leash. A nylon, cotton-webbed, or leather leash are all good choices. Because of its weight and noise, many trainers do not recommend a chain leash. Do not purchase a leash with a large metal clip that is too heavy or uncomfortable for your puppy. You can always buy the leash of your dreams when your puppy is larger.

Pooper Scooper

If your puppy will be confined to a backyard for his bathroom area, a pooper scooper is indispensable. This long-handled tool can make cleaning up much easier and quicker than with a shovel. No dog likes to play or lounge in a dirty yard. Besides being smelly, droppings are prime breeding grounds for flies. Viruses and intestinal parasites are also transmitted through droppings. Furthermore, a young frolicking puppy might accidentally step in his droppings and then track them into the house.

Times are changing and more communities are enacting and enforcing poop scoop laws. When taking your dog for a walk, a plastic bag is the easiest device to clean up after your dog. Place the bag over the dropping, pick up the

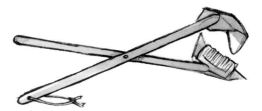

dropping, and then turn the bag inside out. Your hand will always be protected by the plastic bag. Not only is cleanup required in some areas, doing so will win you the appreciation of your neighbors.

Toys

Your puppy needs his own toys, and shopping for puppy toys is fun. An enormous variety of toys are available, but just because they are made for dogs does not mean all of them are safe. By nature, puppies teethe and destroy items, so carefully choose your puppy's toys. Puppies often enjoy carrying around, sleeping with, and thrashing a soft stuffed toy. However, many older puppies are gifted at disemboweling their stuffed toys, potentially swallowing some of the stuffing and even the squeaker. Supervise your puppy's play with any toy that he can

destroy and eat. Sterilized natural bones, nylon bones, and toys made of hard, indestructible rubber are fine for your puppy to chew when he is alone. Rawhide chews of various shapes and sizes are safe for many Weimaraner puppies. However, limit the number you offer if your puppy quickly devours the rawhides (see rawhides for adult dogs page 59).

Too many toys might confuse your puppy as to what items are "his." Limiting the initial number of toys can prevent this. Most puppies enjoy a few hard toys and one soft, stuffed toy. As your puppy grows, you can slowly expand his toy collection. Play with your puppy and his toys but do not play tug-of-war. Doing so encourages your puppy to bite harder and hang on to

It's important for your dog to have a bed that is his own personal space.

A veterinarian makes an important partner in your dog's good health.

items. Not only can this ruin his soft mouth, should you want your Weimaraner as a gun dog, but it is also thought to encourage dominance behavior. Do not encourage your puppy to use his mouth on your hand or clothes; give him a toy instead. Practice saying "give," so that your puppy learns to release his toy to you or other family members. Press on his mouth to make him release his toy as you command "give." Praise him and then give him back his toy.

To the Veterinarian

Ideally, within the first 24 hours, your puppy should be examined by your veterinarian. The veterinarian will check for a spectrum of conditions, including heart murmurs, infections,

bite and teeth alignment, and hernias. If possible, bring a fresh stool sample so your puppy can be checked for internal parasites. This is also the time to discuss with your veterinarian whether any special vaccine products must be ordered, as recommended by the vaccination schedule the breeder gave you (see the section on vaccinations, page 77).

The First Few Nights

You might not sleep soundly the first few nights your puppy is home. For the first week expect to let him sleep in your bedroom inside his crate or a large cardboard sleeping box with the top opened. Later on, you can move his crate or sleeping box into the hall, and then into another room (although Weimaraners are happiest sharing their owners' bedroom). Keeping him next to your bed at night can help your puppy adjust to his new life. You can quietly assure him if he wakes up whimpering and frightened. Persistent crying might indicate that he needs to be taken outside to eliminate. The puppy must adjust to your life, but allowances must be made for his needs. You do not want to encourage 2:00 A.M. play sessions, so after he has voided, return him to his crate. Even if he initially fusses and complains, he will soon fall asleep. Feeding your puppy his last meal of the day earlier in the evening might reduce the need for midnight outings, although your puppy might also just wake up earlier in the morning.

Safety Considerations

You must puppyproof your home. Potentially hazardous items must be removed or moved out of reach.

1. Dispose of poisonous houseplants.

2. Tape electrical cords out of the way.

3. Store household cleaning products and medicines out of reach.

As your puppy follows you about, you might see other areas that need to be altered as you teach your puppy right from wrong.

Puppies explore the world with their mouths and need to chew. Anything left lying on the floor, such as shoes, clothes, books, and so forth, will be tested by your puppy's mouth. These items must be picked up and put out of reach until your puppy knows not to chew them. To a puppy, children's toys can look just like his own. However, seldom are such toys sturdy enough for a puppy. Avoid the temptation to teach children to pick up their toys by letting the puppy destroy a few. If the puppy swallows pieces, they can cause digestive problems and an expensive veterinary bill. Until he knows better, keep an unsupervised puppy out of the children's room and help your youngsters pick up their toys.

Your puppy should not be allowed to roam freely throughout the house. Instead, you should confine your puppy to one or two rooms where you can watch him. Close the doors to the other rooms, and block off access to the rest of the house with inside gates.

The Puppy Room

If you do not use a crate, you must confine your puppy to a safe room within your home. Typically, the kitchen or bathroom are best, because they have tile or linoleum floors that are easy to keep clean. Because you want the puppy to be part of your family, the kitchen is usu-

Puppy-proofing your home means making sure all potentially harmful materials are well out of your dog's reach.

ally best. Be sure the cupboards are securely closed. Move all poisonous products safely out of reach in case your puppy does open a cupboard. Use a temporary gate to keep him in the room.

This method does have disadvantages. Your puppy can wake up before you do and eliminate. Therefore, you will need to either keep him in a cardboard box to minimize this chance or paper train your puppy. While paper training can delay the housebreaking process, it can help to keep things tidier in the interim. Confine your puppy to a small room or partition an area of the room. Make sure the space is large enough so your puppy will not have to eliminate near his bed, food, or water bowls. Cover the floor with newspaper, which you can eventually reduce in coverage as you will find the puppy always uses one spot. This method has disadvantages because it does allow a puppy to eliminate in the house. Furthermore, puppies show great discrimination when it comes to surfaces and might prefer to use newspapers rather than dirt or grass. If this problem develops, place some newspaper on the ground outside.

Life with a Puppy

A Weimaraner puppy is active and playful. He needs plenty of exercise and interactive play and stimulation. At various intervals throughout the day, your puppy will bounce around, wild and rambunctious, and then he will be fast asleep. You want your puppy to learn your rules with a minimum of stress. Have patience and understanding while he is a puppy. Help him channel his energy into acceptable activities so he does not destroy things. Do not encourage behavior in your puppy that would be unacceptable for an adult dog. Now is the time for your puppy to get used to being touched all over, including his mouth, ears, and feet.

Weimaraner puppies are born with brilliant blue eyes that begin to fade around six weeks of age. A puppy's eventual adult eye color will be either light amber, gray, or blue-gray. Between seven to twelve weeks your puppy will be cuddly and dependent on you. Many Weimaraner puppies love being carried and snuggled at this stage, a pleasure they enjoy even after they grow large and gangly. During this time, your puppy has a high learning potential.

Between twelve and sixteen weeks he will assert his own will and become more mischievous and potentially destructive. Because he has a longer attention span, you can train him for longer periods. Adolescence begins around four to five months when the puppy loses his baby teeth. This period can last until the puppy is between seven to nine months of age. Like a moody teenager, your puppy will have days of rebelliousness and insecurity. You might need to reinforce basic obedience commands rather than working on new ones. Be patient—your puppy will eventually grow up.

When you take your puppy outside to play in your fenced backyard, watch him for the first few times. A puppy might eat flowers, shrubs, and lawn furniture, and find other hazards and ways to escape that you might not know about. Some backyard plants are poisonous; if a puppy eats them, he could get sick, and even die. Lists of poisonous plants are available from many references and should be reviewed to make sure toxic plants are not in your yard.

Until your puppy completes his vaccinations, limit his exposure to other dogs and avoid areas where dogs concentrate, such as dog parks. Check with your veterinarian on how soon your puppy can safely socialize with other dogs.

Young puppies have trouble walking up and down stairs. You will need to carry your puppy until he is big enough to safely negotiate stairs on his own. Do not overexert your new puppy even as he grows in size and becomes more exuberant. Your Weimaraner should not accompany you on runs or bike rides until he is at least a year old. Check with your veterinarian for the appropriate age to increase his exercise regimen. Many veterinarians think stressing the joints of a growing puppy through excessive exercise can increase the potential for future joint problems.

Children and the Puppy

Both children and a puppy must learn how to behave around one another. As is true of any breed, Weimaraner puppies have sharp teeth that can frighten children if they play-bite. Puppies tend to jump and their sharp nails can scratch unprotected skin. As a Weimaraner puppy grows bigger, he can accidentally knock over or hurt a small child.

An adult should supervise the puppy and children to be sure they interact safely and appropriately. Children must learn not to encourage the puppy to run after them, and the puppy must learn not to chase and jump on children. Do not allow children to be rough or allow the puppy to nip. If your puppy is teething, have the children give him a toy on which to gnaw, not their hands or clothes. Children sometimes tease a puppy by wiggling their fingers in front of the puppy's face or by taking away a toy and then repeatedly tempting him with it. Children must be taught not to tease the puppy.

Car Travel

Most Weimaraners like to travel with people in the car. Car trips are easier if your dog does not get anxious, carsick, or unruly. Start teaching your puppy when he is young how to ride in the car. Discourage him from barking, and do not let him run among the seats or hang his head out the window. Some Weimaraners naturally sit quietly and enjoy looking out the windows. Others must be taught good car manners. A variety of harness restraints are available that

Be sure not to overexert your puppy as he grows in size.

Young Weimaraners are full of energy and need plenty of active playtime.

allow your dog to safely and securely ride in the car. If your car is large enough, your dog can also safely travel in his crate.

Take your puppy on short errands to get him used to riding in the car. If you occasionally schedule a stop at a park where he can play or you let him out to visit an admirer, he will be even happier to go. To prevent a potential accident, teach your puppy not to bolt from the car. He should learn to wait until you give the command to jump in or out. Leaving a hard chew bone when your puppy is alone in the car will give him something to do while he waits for your return.

Be aware of outside temperatures when you leave your dog alone in the car. The temperature inside a car can become hot, even when the windows are open and the car is parked in the shade. The glass hatchbacks of some cars also cause the car to rapidly heat up. On cold, snowy days it is not beneath your Weimaraner's dignity to wear a dog sweater when he must wait in the car.

Weimaraners are a relatively easy breed to housebreak, but keep several points in mind. Some puppies are easy to house-train. They make no mistakes and within a few days, they stand by the door when they need to go outside. Others take longer. House-breaking can be more difficult to accomplish if you are at work all day. The more you are present, the greater the chance you will recognize when your puppy needs to go outside.

A crate will make house-training your new puppy easier and more effective. By keeping your puppy in his crate when you cannot watch him, you help prevent accidents in the house. Use of a crate reduces house-training time to a minimum. Avoiding the need to continually correct the puppy for making mistakes reduces the stress for both of you.

Consistency is the key, as with any type of training. You will need to take your puppy outside several times a day. Puppies have four typical times they need to eliminate:

✔ When they first wake up in the morning.

✔ Immediately after eating each meal.

✔ About fifteen minutes after playtime.

✔ Just before bedtime.

Develop a schedule for your puppy so he is taken out at these same times each day. Along with a regular elimination schedule, feeding your puppy at consistent times will make house-training easier.

When you wake up in the morning, the first thing you need to do is take your puppy outside. For the first week or two, you might need to carry your puppy to avoid the chance of an accident happening on the way outside. Give the command "outside" as you leave the house. Set him down in the same place each time. Do not leave him outside by himself. You must make sure that he does his business. Stand quietly while you wait for him to go, which sometimes can take a while. Use a "bathroom" command such as "go pee," and praise him when he eliminates. Then take him back inside.

If he does not go in a few minutes, take him back inside. Do not let him stay outside to play. This helps him learn that the outdoors is for elimination. Keep the bathroom area clean of droppings; however, the smell of urine will encourage your puppy to use the spot.

Put him in his crate each evening to reduce the chance of accidents, but be sure he has eliminated before crating. Taking your puppy outside late at night can help him sleep through the night. If your puppy wakes up whimpering, chances are he has to go outside.

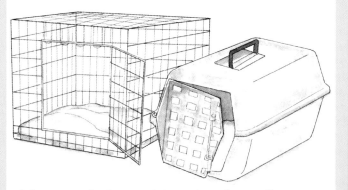

A dog crate makes house-training easier and more effective.

How can you tell when your puppy needs to eliminate? When puppies need to urinate, they often stop and squat with little warning. To prevent accidents, use timing. How long was it since your puppy last went outside? If it is more than a few hours, take him outside and praise him when he goes. When puppies need to defecate, their behavior changes. They suddenly stop playing and begin to sniff around. Some might circle around and around in preparation to eliminate. Be watchful for these behaviors. If necessary, quickly scoop up your puppy and take him outside. Be alert; your puppy might stand by the door when he needs to go outside.

The best method to house-train your puppy: Do not give your puppy the opportunity to make a mistake in the house. With house-training, you must think for your puppy. You need to keep track of how long it has been since your puppy last went outside. A young puppy cannot "hold it" for more than a couple of hours after he has already eliminated. A puppy between three to four months old can often contain himself for four hours, although he will be unhappy if left that long in his crate. If you are vigilant, you should know before your puppy does when he needs to go. Therefore, you will have few accidents to clean and your puppy will give fewer reasons to be scolded.

If you catch your puppy in the act of making a mistake, use a firm "No," loud enough to startle him, but do not yell at him. Do not get angry and scare your puppy. Pulling or pushing

If you catch your pup in the act, get down to his level and give a firm verbal scolding.

your puppy hurriedly out the door will not stop the puppy from going and will only frighten him. Pick up your puppy, take him outside to his bathroom area and give his bathroom command. Praise him for going outside and then bring him back inside again.

If you discover a mistake your puppy already has made, do not yell at him or push his nose into the mess. Because of the time lapse he will not understand why you are yelling at him, and such methods can derail the house-training process and create more problems. His accident is your mistake because you did not pay enough attention. After you clean up the mess, use an odor-neutralizing product sold at pet stores. This will remove any scent that might attract your puppy to the same place.

TRAINING

Why?

Puppies naturally love people, but they do not know how to live in people's homes or interact with people in an acceptable manner. A puppy does not know the rules, and must be taught how to behave and what is right and wrong. For your Weimaraner puppy to develop into the canine companion of your dreams, he needs formal training to channel his instincts and energy into agreeable behavior.

Training lets your Weimaraner know what is expected of him and will not break his spirit. Dogs who are trained are secure and confident, because they know where they fit in a family's structure and in human society. Training enables an undisciplined, obnoxious dog to learn acceptable ways to get attention. Dogs who are shy and insecure become more confident. Dominant dogs learn that you are the boss. The pride and enthusiasm you will feel in having a well-trained dog requires a commitment of time and energy spent training.

When most people get a puppy, they think it will be for the lifetime of the dog. However, the unexpected does happen and for a variety of reasons, sometimes people have to relinquish their dog. It is much easier for you or for a rescue group or shelter to find your dog a new home if he is trained, socialized, and well mannered. People sometimes give up their dogs because of bad behavior; the commitment to formal training can help prevent this possibility.

The Leader

A dog's wild canine relatives, such as wolves, are pack animals. To live in a pack successfully, there must be a pecking order, so that each animal knows where he and the other members fit in the hierarchy. The animal at the top of the hierarchy is the dominant or alpha individual, also known as the leader.

The leader controls the activities of the pack and typically initiates activities such as hunting. The other wolves watch carefully and follow the alpha's lead. The pack leader gets first choice at any food, can sleep anywhere he likes, goes first through any opening or into any new territory, and can demand attention anytime.

Your dog is also a pack animal and you are his wise and benevolent leader, never capricious or cruel. Obedience training in dogs operates on this premise. Like a good pack member, your dog will learn to take directions from you. You give your dog the rules and conditions to live by, which give him confidence about his position. Your Weimaraner should be a happy, lower-ranked member of your family pack who is willing to accept your commands and control, as well as those of all other family members. You must act like a leader and enforce your role. For example, your dog must not only

Weimaraner pups are inquisitive and very playful.

obey you, he must not rush out the door ahead of you, and he must relinquish a toy or bone to you when asked.

When to Begin Training

Begin training as soon your puppy enters your home. As long as you are clear on what is and is not allowed, your puppy will learn quickly. A basic rule of dog training is that it is easier to prevent problems than it is to fix them. A puppy is just a baby and should not be expected to be always on his best Sunday behavior. Let him be a puppy, but direct and encourage behaviors that are desirable for an adult dog. Do not encourage behaviors that will be difficult to tolerate in an adult.

Basic obedience classes are important. In some areas, these are called puppy kindergarten. Most Weimaraner puppies are capable of beginning formal obedience class when they are nine weeks old (provided the instructor requires proof that all canines are either vaccinated or on a vaccination schedule). In a class with older dogs, it is often the puppies that learn the best. A solid foundation in basic obedience commands will make your puppy's rebellious adolescent stage easier.

Short Sessions

Puppies have a short concentration time, but long memories. Outside of class, keep your training sessions short and integrate numerous short sessions into daily life. For example, tell your puppy to sit before each meal. When working on a command, do not practice for so long that your puppy loses interest and is bored. Executing a command two to three times is often enough. Weimaraners, like people, find repetition boring. Always end a training session on a positive note while your puppy is still interested and has performed a command well. Resist the urge to ask for the command one additional time. Train your puppy both when he is on his best behavior and when he is ornery—obedience is not limited just to your puppy's good times. Work with your puppy to build his confidence and trust in your authority. As your puppy matures, training sessions can lengthen and incorporate more commands.

Your puppy will take some time to learn simple commands, such as sit and stay. Yet as he matures, the more you train your puppy, the faster he will learn to learn, and the more easily you will be able to teach additional commands.

Tone of Voice

Your tone of voice should reflect your leadership role. Firmly give a command only once, and then, if necessary, enforce it. Avoid giving commands such as "come on, sit down." Your commands should be clear and concise, and the puppy should have no doubt what you mean (for example, "*sit*" or "*down*"). Use one-word commands. Do not whine, cajole, or plead, "please, come on, sit down." This tone of voice can communicate distress to your dog, since it sounds like whimpering; at the very least it is not clear and forceful.

Tip: Change the tone of your voice when you give a verbal correction. If your puppy still does not respond, issue the correction in a firmer, growling tone.

Timing

When to give praise or a correction is very important. In order for your puppy to associate his behavior with your response, your praise or correction must be given when his behavior is occurring (within three seconds!).

Dogs do not have a human conception of time. Your dog will not remember that five minutes ago he was chewing on the leg of a chair. Therefore, he will not associate your anger with his previous actions. However, in response to your upset demeanor (even if you think you are not giving out any signals), he will lower his body and eyes and put back his ears, giving the appearance of guilt. Most animal behaviorists agree; dogs do not feel guilt, spite, or other negative human emotions that are often attributed to them, most notably when they have been bad.

Because dogs are such familiar animals, it can be difficult for some people to respect and remember that dogs are a different species, with a different approach to learning than our own.

Aversion Tools

Sometimes a puppy is so thoroughly engaged in an activity, he appears not to hear the word "no." When "no" is not enough to dissuade your puppy from pulling on the curtains or gnawing on the leg of a chair, you can use an aversion tool—a shake can (soda can filled with pennies or pebbles), a small water pistol, a whistle, or even loudly clapping your hands together can be used as aversion tools. The purpose of an aversion tool is to break your puppy's concentration so that he stops what he is doing. Just as with the command "no," when your puppy looks up, you must redirect him from the activity in which he was engaged and then praise him for doing right.

Timing is important. You must use the aversion method when your puppy is engaged in the undesired behavior, not after he has already released the curtains or stopped chewing the chair leg. Rather than searching for where you left a whistle or shake can, clapping your hands together often works best. Do not overuse an aversion tool. It is a method of last resort. Nor should you use it in a threatening manner. Its purpose is to startle, but not scare your puppy, so you can redirect him to an acceptable behavior.

Positive Reinforcement

There are many training methods, all with their sworn adherents, and you will discover plenty of dog owners quick to offer unsolicited advice as to the best way to train your puppy. While more than one method can work, the best method for your Weimaraner relies on positive treatment and reinforcement of desired behaviors. This method uses praise, such as a small tidbit of food or your voice, and correction, not punishment, to achieve the desired behavior.

In urban areas, there are usually many choices when it comes to selecting a dog trainer and class. Avoid classes and trainers that use harsh or physical treatment. Such methods are not necessary with the Weimaraner. Neither should you ever hit your Weimaraner. This breed is highly sensitive; anger, force, or physical punishment can make them headshy and unwilling to work with you. Do not develop an adversarial relationship with your Weimaraner. You are both on the same team. Weimaraners have good memories, and it can be a lot of work to win back their high regard. Even documents from more than 100 years ago note that the Weimaraner is sensitive and could be ruined by the slightest

mistreatment; it was an accepted rule to treat the Weimaraner well and lovingly.

A Consistent Standard

You must take the leadership role with your Weimaraner. If you do not, your Weimaraner will have you living according to his terms, not yours. This will create a bad situation for all when your

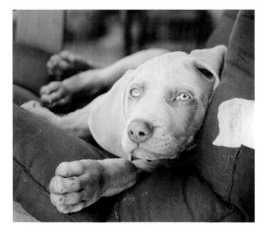

Weimaraners are affectionate dogs.

puppy becomes full-grown. As your puppy matures, and in particular, when an adolescent, he will occasionally try to challenge your authority. You must not ignore his challenges. To many people, these challenges can be subtle, but most start with the ignored command.

Never give your dog a command that you are not prepared or able to enforce. This means you do not "lazily" request your dog to sit, and when he does not comply, you ignore his disobedience. It takes a certain energy and alertness to enforce a command. If you are not going to follow through, do not give your puppy a command. You must know before you give a command that you mean it. Such situations occur less frequently in a structured setting, such as obedience class or when you are practicing your puppy's lessons. They are most likely to happen within your home when you are busy and distracted. This is when it matters most, because this is how your puppy will share your home. Many Weimaraners are savvy to home life and learn there are situations when you are unlikely to correct them, such as when you are talking on the phone or eating dinner. To prevent your dog from becoming obnoxious, excuse yourself for a moment and rectify the situation. Otherwise your dog is on the path to commander-in-chief.

As your puppy's leader, you must be consistent and persistent and enforce your commands and rules. Doing so can be hard work, but is ultimately worth it. You must be alert

Although rugged and athletic, Weimaraners are also creatures of comfort.

Housebreaking your pet will take time and patience.

and pay attention to your puppy, even when you are tired or your puppy's misbehavior is cute. Sometimes it will seem easier to ignore half-bad behavior than to correct it. However, if you give your puppy an inch it can sometimes lead to a mile. Erratic, unpredictable enforcement will confuse your puppy and can lead to his testing your authority.

Training Equipment

A flat-buckle collar is usually sufficient for your puppy's first six months of training. When he reaches his adolescent stage and becomes a bit rebellious, you should then purchase a chain or nylon choke collar. Be careful when using the choke collar. A Weimaraner does not have thick fur to protect his throat against abuse. A choke collar works with a quick "pop," not by yanking and spinning your puppy around or by sustained pulling. In addition to a 6-foot (180 cm) leash, a retractable leash or drag line (at least 20 feet (6–7 m) long) is needed. These longer leads help you to practice and enforce obedience commands when your puppy is farther away from you.

Value of Obedience Classes

Many people who have previously owned dogs forego obedience classes because they think they can do the job themselves. In many cases they can. However, obedience classes are valuable for a number of other reasons. Classes provide a forum for training not easily replicated by an owner with a single puppy. In a

class, your puppy has the opportunity to socialize with other dogs and people. He will learn how to control his response to distractions and learn to obey you in the presence of other dogs and people. Naturally, it helps that the other dogs are also under control.

Your puppy learns basic obedience and good manners; you learn how to train your puppy. The class instructor should have the expertise to help *you* learn to train (and communicate with) your puppy. Much of a dog's potential has to do with the person training the dog. A good, smart dog can be ruined by someone who does not know what he or she is doing. The benefits of a good obedience class include the assistance of someone experienced in working with a wide variety of dogs and situations. An instructor is invaluable when you run into a problem and cannot figure out how to solve it. Instead of feeling ruffled, the instructor can help you remedy the situation.

Your dog should not "flunk out" of obedience class, nor should you give up before the course is completed. If you feel frustrated or make poor progress, investigate whether private lessons or another class is available. (The problem with sending your dog off to training school is that you, the human, need to learn almost as much as your puppy.)

A trainer can help you:

1. Figure out *how* to teach your puppy or dog without losing your patience or resorting to aggressive threats or punishment. Thus, your dog's trust in you will not be undermined. A trainer has the experience to help shortcut frustrating routines and to give you encouragement in your progress.

2. Discover any problems in your techniques so you can be more effective. For example, a trainer can assist you with your timing so you reward or correct your dog at the right time.

3. Recognize behaviors in your puppy that you otherwise would not, such as dominant or fearful tendencies. The class instructor should have the skills to teach you how to change or manage your dog's behavior.

4. Establish yourself as your dog's ruler. He is the commanded, you are the commander; he is the ruled, you are the ruler; he is the follower, you are the leader. Formal obedience class gives you a framework for establishing leadership with, or dominance over, your dog.

5. Adhere to a regular training schedule. Sometimes when people get too busy, they slack off or completely skip important things like puppy training. However, when a class with specific lessons on which to work is scheduled once a week, pet owners are often motivated to find the time to work on lessons.

6. Illustrate *how* to consistently train your puppy for each specific command. Since you will have been shown how to get your dog to understand a command, it is easier and less frustrating

to practice. In addition, you will know which commands to practice at what times.

Family Members

Along with the puppy's primary owner or caretaker, all family members should take turns attending the puppy's obedience classes, including children who are at least elementary school age. This will help the whole family use consistent training methods and commands. Family members who do not help to train the puppy often issue a variety of conflicting and confusing instructions. The puppy becomes stressed when faced with inconsistent demands that he does not understand and ends up ignoring everyone but the person who trained him.

Basic Obedience Commands

Sit, *Down*, *Stay*, *Come*, and *Heel* are the five simple obedience commands every dog needs to obey in order to make him a pleasant companion with whom to share your life. If you go on to advanced training, you will teach your dog to respond to hand signals and additional commands.

Always train your puppy on a leash so you have control over him. Without a leash you have no way of enforcing your commands, and your Weimaraner puppy might get bored and walk away or have the impression that he does not have to listen to you. The only way a puppy learns to obey commands is to realize that once given, commands must be obeyed. Give a command only once before enforcing it. You want your Weimaraner to respond to "*stay*," not to "stay, stay, stay." Once your puppy responds reflexively to your commands in a variety of situations and circumstances, then you can begin to practice each command off leash.

Undoubtedly, the instructor for the obedience class in which you enroll your puppy will have a preferred method for teaching the basic commands. However, in some areas, classes are not available or they do not accept puppies younger than a certain age, such as six months. Your puppy is extremely receptive to learning between seven and twelve weeks of age; do not waste this time just because no class is available. The following methods of teaching the basic commands work well, and you are certainly encouraged to follow up with additional commands, with help from training books and local dog clubs.

Your puppy will not always think you are wonderful and fascinating. For the first few weeks, your puppy will naturally want to stay close to you. But within a few weeks, your puppy will be more confident and independent, at which point he might hesitate before deciding whether to respond to your commands.

Teaching your puppy to establish eye contact with you can help to keep his attention focused on you. Eye contact is a form of dominance. Do not "lose" by being the first to break eye contact. Using a small food treat held near your eyes, tell your puppy "watch me" and reward him when he looks in your eyes. Eventually, move the treat away from your face, and reward your puppy with it when he looks in your eyes, not at the treat.

Proper use of food treats is important. When the puppy is first learning a command, immediately praise and give a food treat when your puppy has done what you wanted. Once your puppy has learned a command, you will switch and randomly reward him with the treat or praise. Your puppy will perform his best if he does not know when to expect a treat or praise. As his repertoire of learned commands increases, you will reward him with a food treat only for learning new commands, not for performing the ones he should already know. Eventually, you will not use food treats at all. For more complicated commands, a chance to play a game of fetch might be an effective reward for some dogs.

The Command "No"

Inevitably, your puppy will learn the command "*No!*" shortly after he comes into your home. Do not frighten your puppy into learning this command. Just say it loud enough for him to hear, and then give him something else to do, or put him out of harm's way. Avoid overusing this command; your puppy should not think his name ends or begins with "no." If you see your puppy heading toward mischief, head him off and give him something acceptable to do.

Release Command

Of absolute importance is a release command. This command lets your puppy know he can break the previous command and resume doing what he wants. Many owners make the mistake of telling their dog to sit or lie down and then they forget about their dog. Eventually the dog gets up and moves. Sometimes, the owner yells at the dog for moving, but other times the owner ignores the dog. This inconsistency is confusing to the dog.

Therefore, never give a command without also knowing that you want your dog to break it only when you "release" him. For example, when you command your puppy to sit, you will let him know he can get up from the sit when

Most Weimaraners learn the "sit" command quickly when you push down gently on their hindquarters.

you give the release command. If at first your puppy does not seem to understand the release command, get him excited and he will break his position.

The word "OK" is not the best choice for a release command because it is often used in everyday conversation. If your dog is sitting at your side while you are talking to someone, and you use the word "OK" in the conversation, your dog will probably break his sit. If you are in a busy location and your dog is not on a leash, this could have bad consequences. For this reason, many trainers prefer *"release!"* or *"break!"*

Sit

Many Weimaraner puppies quickly learn this command after only a few repetitions. Give the command *"sit"* and gently push down on your puppy's hindquarters until he sits. Immediately praise him. Alternatively, show him a treat, then raise it above his head so that he natu-

rally moves into the sitting position. When he does, say *"sit"* and give the treat. Have him sit for a few seconds, then give your release command so he can get up. When you have his attention again, repeat the lesson. If your puppy tries to get up before the release command, pull up on the leash so he sits again, or if necessary push down on his hindquarters. Praise him, then release him.

Down

Once your puppy knows how to sit, you can teach him *"down."* First have your puppy sit. Then show him a treat and move the treat down and forward until it is in front of his paws. The puppy should move into the down position. When he does, say *"down"* and reward him. If necessary, gently push down on his shoulders. He may get back up after you give the release command. Some puppies do not like the down command because it puts them in a subordinate position.

Stay

After your puppy has mastered "*sit*" and "*down*" you will teach him the command "*stay*" while he is in the down position. Command your puppy to "*down*," then put your palm forward, in front of his face and say "*stay*." Stand up and step back a few paces. Move slowly and wait a few seconds before returning to your puppy. Put your foot on the leash so your puppy cannot jump up when you get closer. Praise your puppy for staying, give him a treat, and then release him.

If your puppy gets up before you release him, put him back in the down position without scolding and start again. Gradually increase the distance you go from your puppy. After he "*stays*" with you standing in front of him, slowly circle around him. Hold the leash and let it slide through your hand so you can exert pressure should your puppy try to get up. An instructor is useful when you are teaching "*stay*" and increasing your distance from your puppy. If your puppy tries to follow you, the instructor can quickly correct him. (The puppy might perceive your running back to correct him as a reward for breaking his "*stay*.") Aim to teach your puppy to "*stay*" when you are out of his sight and for up to ten minutes. But proceed slowly and very gradually.

Teaching the "stay" command.

Come

"*Come*" means your dog quickly comes directly to you, looks at you, and waits for further instruction. This is an essential command that can save your dog's life and save you from yelling yourself hoarse. It is very important that

Most Weimaraners will tolerate cats if they grow up together.

when you teach this command you are able to enforce it. When starting a training program, do not use "*come*" if you cannot make your puppy respond. Only give the command if you have a 6-foot (180 cm) or a retractable leash attached to your puppy. Give the command only once, and if your puppy does not pay attention, give the leash a quick pop. Open your arms, bend down, be enthusiastic and your puppy will respond. Lavishly praise or give a treat to your puppy for coming when called, then release him and repeat the exercise.

A few caveats: Start training from short distances—5 feet (150 cm)—and progress to longer distances using the retractable leash or drag line. Practice the command in a variety of situations. Once your puppy consistently responds to the command when he is on leash, you can practice training him off leash. Do not run after your puppy if he ignores you; instead call his name and slowly jog away from him (he cannot resist the invitation to pursue you). Call him only when there is a high likelihood that he will respond (when he is not doing something more interesting). Finally, never yell at him for (eventually) coming.

Many times when people have their dog off leash and they want the dog to range closer to them, they give the command "*come*." The dog proceeds toward them, but then veers away or stops short of the owner. Since the owner wanted the dog in closer, which is what the dog did, the owner overlooks the fact that the dog did not come to him or her. Eventually, the command "*come*" erodes into "come closer to me, but you don't have to come to me." To prevent this, use another command, such as "*yip*," "*here*," or a unique whistle, when you want your dog to range in closer to you. Save

"*come*" for when you mean "*come to me*" and practice how it should be performed.

Heel

When you are walking your 70-pound Weimaraner on a leash, he is supposed to keep pace with you, not charge ahead dragging you along. It is easiest to teach the "*heel*" command when your dog is a puppy. "*Heel*" is the command you will use to teach your puppy to walk on a loose leash, without pulling. You must first train your puppy to "*line up*" on your left side. Standing in front of your puppy, use a food treat to move him behind your back and into a sitting position at your left side. Give the command "*line up*" and reward him.

From this position, you will purposefully move forward with your left leg and give the command "*heel*." If your puppy bolts ahead of you, do a 180-degree turn and move in the opposite direction. Enough surprise turns will teach him that you are the leader and he has to pay attention and follow you. For best results, continue to practice this as your puppy grows and develops, and eventually train it in different locations.

Other Useful Commands

Leave It

Teach your puppy this command when he is in the "*down-stay*" position. Place several food treats on the ground just out of the puppy's reach and say "*leave it*." Stand on the leash should he try to strain forward. Wait a minute and then say "*good leave-it*" and reward him with a different treat. This command is useful for teaching your puppy to leave garbage, animal droppings, and even some people alone.

Give

"*Give*" usually means your puppy delivers and places into your hand an object that is in his mouth. Practice "*give*" with your puppy's bones and toys. As the leader, you have the right to take away your puppy's toys or chews. Calmly and gently say "*give*" and firmly take away the object. Do not let your puppy grab it back. Praise your puppy and then give him back his toy or bone. Incorporating play will reward your puppy for giving you the object. The reward does not always have to be a food treat.

Drop It

The command "*drop it*" means your puppy drops onto the ground whatever he has in his mouth. Teach your puppy this command by gently opening his mouth so he drops the object. Say "*drop it*" and then praise him. This is useful when your puppy has something disgusting like a dead animal or feces in his mouth and you do not want to touch it.

Out

This command is useful if you want your puppy to stay out of a certain room. Your tone of voice, stance, and demeanor should indicate what you want.

Socialization

Socialization occurs when you expose your puppy to new environments, such as parks, shops, noisy schoolyards, and friends' homes, and you introduce him to as many new people as possible of all ages and sizes. As long as he is calm and happy, socialization helps your puppy learn to get along with others and provides your puppy with positive experiences so he does not become shy or fearful. Socialization will help to prevent potential future problems and is as important for your Weimaraner as basic obedience training. The peak socialization opportunity ends around twelve weeks of age, so be sure to perform this exercise well before that age.

Because of the risk of infection to a puppy who has not completed his vaccinations, check with your veterinarian and breeder about the safest age to take your puppy to new places. You should continue to socialize your puppy as he grows and matures. While your puppy is young, he should meet whatever might be part of his future life. Do let him meet friendly dogs who have current vaccinations.

For safety and control, keep your puppy on a leash during these excursions. Make your excursions positive experiences. Reassure your puppy if he becomes scared, but do so with happy, bold words to encourage his confidence.

Seek socialization situations for your puppy while he still young. If you do not have children, take your puppy to a park on the weekend. Let him smell, see, and hear children running and playing. Most people like meeting puppies and young dogs. Parents will bring over their children to visit or a child might ask if he can pet your puppy. It is best if your puppy already knows how to sit so that he is under control.

Since a Weimaraner puppy is irresistible, have some small pieces of dog biscuit a child can offer to your puppy who is sitting. Be prepared to correct the puppy if he tries to jump or get unruly. Because young puppies still have sharp teeth and might grab, the child can offer the treat on a flat hand. Children and adults are usually receptive and patient if you tell them your puppy is in training and learning how to behave properly.

CARE OF THE ADULT WEIMARANER

Routine

Dogs like routine. If you take your Weimaraner out for a walk every morning at 7:00 A.M., he will expect the same on weekends, and he will start to get fidgety around that time. Weimaraners are most comfortable with the rules they grow up with and are somewhat resistant to change. Practice flexible scheduling while your Weimaraner is still young so he will be more adaptable.

Exercising Your Dog

Weimaraners are an intelligent, versatile breed capable of doing many things. The more interaction you have with your dog, the more he will respond, the more you will enjoy him, and the better memories you will create. The first seven years of your Weimaraner's life can be characterized by "Go, go, go." This will not change much until your dog approaches his senior years. Giving your dog enough exercise is important. When you start your dog on an exercise regimen, start slowly, and build up his condition to longer distances, just as you would for yourself. If you bike, several products are available that allow you to safely bike with your dog. The dog is clipped to an attachment on the bike,

Although less energetic, your older Weimaraner still needs a daily walk.

which allows you to keep both hands on the handlebars.

Weimaraners have webbed feet and naturally love to swim. As puppies, most Weimaraners will eventually enter the water on their own, or they will follow another dog or you into the water and thus learn to swim. Never throw your puppy into the water to make him swim. Doing so is traumatic and can make him hate water. Oceans are large and threatening, and the water tastes bad. They are not the best place for a timid puppy to become acquainted with swimming. As long as it is warm enough, your Weimaraner will eagerly swim. (Some individual dogs even swim when it is freezing outside, but without a thick coat, they will shiver when they get out of the water.) Retrieving a thrown ball or stick in a lake or pond is a great way to help your Weimaraner expend energy.

Behavior Problems

Barking

Although not known as excessive barkers, a Weimaraner given inadequate exercise and attention can develop into a nuisance barker who barks because he is lonely and bored. If you are not home during the day to correct this behavior, it can develop into a problem.

If necessary, several devices to inhibit barking, such as collars that squirt citronella oil or administer a small shock, can be used. However, the loneliness, boredom, or other underlying reasons for the barking must be addressed.

Separation Anxiety

When a Weimaraner is left alone, barking and destructive behavior are typical symptoms of separation anxiety. Some dogs become so agitated they might try to escape from the yard or destroy furniture. Most Weimaraners bond closely with their owners and do not like being alone, but they do not develop separation anxiety.

Introduce your puppy to separations by keeping the intervals brief and varying the length of time so your puppy will not know how long he will be by himself. Make your departures and returns low-key and your puppy will not feel anxious. Keeping your puppy in his crate for your absences is one method of preventing this behavior from developing.

For a dog that already has separation anxiety, the typical treatment involves desensitizing the dog to your leaving the house. Pretend you are leaving by picking up keys and coat and leaving for a few minutes and then returning. Next, wait outside the door a little longer and at the first sign of misbehavior open the door and yell "No!" and then leave. When your dog has been quiet, reenter the house and praise him. You will gradually work up to absences of several hours. If given adequate exercise and a routine schedule, separation anxiety will sometimes go away by itself. Try keeping your dog busy with an enjoyable activity while you are gone. Coat the inside of a hollow bone with peanut butter and then freeze the bone. Give the frozen treat to your dog before you leave; it will keep him occupied for a long time.

If necessary, medication can be used as a last resort for treatment of separation anxiety. Consult with your veterinarian, who can evaluate your dog. The prescribed medication can be used to break the cycle of separation anxiety, with the ultimate goal of gradually weaning your dog from the medication.

Jumping

Friendly dogs and puppies jump up on people as a form of greeting, especially when they are happy and excited. However, it can be annoying when your dog jumps up, especially if you are dressed nicely, or if your dog jumps on guests. It can also be dangerous when an adult Weimaraner jumps on children or elderly people.

As is true of most things, it is much easier to prevent this habit from developing in a puppy, than it is to train an adult dog not to jump. You can use several methods to prevent or correct this problem. Crouch down when greeting your puppy so he does not have to jump. Calmly greet your puppy; do not get excited upon seeing him. Redirect your puppy's enthusiasm by distracting him with something else, such as tossing one of his toys. Because jumping up is self-rewarding, teach your puppy that jumping will be ignored. If he jumps on you, step back or turn aside so he cannot make contact, and ignore him until all four feet are on the ground. When your puppy jumps, firmly state "No!" Give the command "Off!" followed by the command "Sit." When he complies, then visit and praise him. If necessary, holding and squeezing your dog's paws for one or two minutes while you look away is effective.

Note: Kneeing a dog in the chest can cause serious internal injuries and is not recommended.

A Word on Breeding

As a breed, Weimaraners have already suffered from unscrupulous breeding as a result of their popularity. Any time a breed receives publicity, whether because of movies, commercials, or artwork, a breed increases in popularity and people think of breeding their pets to fill the demand.

Many people are afflicted with the "my dog is unique" syndrome. Thinking your dog has the best looks, brains, and temperament is great, but it does not mean your dog should produce offspring. In particular, owners of unneutered male dogs seem to feel their dogs are unique and worthy of siring a litter (probably because they will not have the work involved with the puppies). However, your opinions regarding your dog's qualities are not sufficient criteria for deciding whether to breed him or her. Reread the section (page 30) on what a reputable breeder does to produce quality puppies (for example, screen for genetic disorders). Such breeders will continue to produce wonderful dogs without any contribution from yours.

A reasonable time to consider breeding is after your dog has distinguished himself or herself in show or field trials, or as a personal gun dog. Then you will find an experienced breeder who is willing to mentor you.

Spaying and Neutering

Spaying refers to removal of the female dog's ovaries and uterus. The male dog is neutered, which refers to the removal of the male's testicles. Unless you plan to breed your dog as part of a conscientious breeding program, you should fix him or her. Your dog's activity level and personality will not change after this procedure.

Female dogs who are spayed before their first heat cycle, which can occur between seven to twenty-four months of age, have a lesser risk of developing mammary cancer. The number of mixed-breed puppies born every year are a testament to the old saying regarding a female in heat, "Board the windows, bolt the doors, block the chimney, keep her inside for three weeks, and expect puppies in 63 days." Once spayed, a female will not have a twice-yearly, 21-day messy heat cycle, nor can she become pregnant.

Male dogs are usually not neutered until they are about one year old. Neutering can decrease a male's dominance aggression toward other unneutered males.

Because of the high incidence of reproductive disorders in older dogs, most veterinarians recommend neutering, and most breeders neuter their dogs by their eighth birthday. By having this procedure performed, age-related diseases and infections in older females can be avoided and the incidence of prostate disorders in older males can be reduced.

Toys and Bones

Your dog will continue to play with and enjoy the same types of toys he had as a puppy, although they might need to be larger in size. Bones are necessary to keep your dog's gums and teeth healthy and clean and to provide a healthy outlet for his need to chew. However, now that he is an adult you might notice that he quickly devours his rawhide bones. Some Weimaraners are voracious chewers and gulp down chunks of hooves or bolt pieces of rawhide. This can cause intestinal upset and blockages, which might even require surgical removal. If your dog is this type, avoid offering cow hooves and rawhide chews. When a rawhide becomes slimy and small enough for your dog to swallow, discard and replace it. Some types of rawhide, such as pressed rawhide, last longer because they are denser and not as easily chewed and swallowed. Supervise him when he chews to determine if there is a problem. Other chewing options include nylabones and large marrow bones. Do not give your dog any small bones, which usually include any from your family dinner. It is always better to be safe than sorry.

Boarding Kennels

Finding a good boarding kennel is important if you travel a lot and must leave your dog behind. Some veterinary hospitals have boarding facilities, or your veterinarian can refer you to suitable kennels. Always inspect a new boarding kennel before you leave your dog. The kennel should require that all dogs have current vaccines, including bortadella (kennel cough). Make sure your dog will have his own run, be given attention, and time to play in a securely fenced area. Some Weimaraners become anxious, mope, and refuse to eat when left at a kennel. If you expect to make regular use of a kennel, acclimate your Weimaraner to the kennel and your absences while he is still a puppy; leave him overnight even if it is not necessary. Many dogs are comforted by an owner's smelly shirt or sock and a favorite toy. Swapping dog care with a friend is another suitable option.

Air Travel

For air travel, your dog will need an airline-approved crate. If your dog is not used to a crate, you must acclimate him to the carrier before he flies. Try to book nonstop flights to avoid a lot of ground time when your dog flies. Airlines charge less if you fly on the same flight as your dog. Make sure your dog is wearing his identification tags and provide him with water.

The Senior Dog

A Weimaraner's life expectancy is about twelve years. Generally, Weimaraners are

For air travel, an airline-approved dog crate is a necessity.

Older Weimaraners are happiest when they get to share in the family's activities.

considered senior dogs when they are seven years of age. Because many Weimaraners remain active well into their early teen years, it is often hard for owners to believe their dog is geriatric. Old age sometimes seems to creep up because some of the signs, such as a graying muzzle, are not obvious in many Weimaraners.

Whether or not an owner can detect obvious signs of age, the dog's body is still aging. Your Weimaraner should have annual or biannual wellness checks that can help to detect ailments in their early stages. Your veterinarian might also recommend an annual blood profile and urinalysis to detect disorders of the kidneys and liver.

Older dogs sleep longer and more deeply. Most are more comfortable sleeping on a thick foam orthopedic bed designed to relieve the stress of arthritis and stiff joints. Even though less active, older Weimaraners must still exercise, such as walks around the block. A moderate exercise regimen will help keep your dog's muscles toned, his joints flexible, and his bones strong.

Because senior dogs are less active, their caloric intake must be correspondingly reduced to prevent weight gain. Obesity increases the risk of heart disease and puts more stress on the older dog's joints. An older dog who loses his appetite might need his teeth cleaned. Swollen gums and loose teeth can make eating painful. Anesthesia, which is required for professional cleaning, is riskier for older dogs, so be diligent about brushing your dog's teeth. Older Weimaraners sometimes develop nonmalignant fatty or fibrous skin tumors. These do not usually need to be removed except for cosmetic reasons.

A dog's sense of hearing and sight can decline with age, as can mental alertness. Senior Weimaraners become less emotionally flexible and are easily traumatized if left in unfamiliar surroundings such as a veterinary hospital or kennel.

Saying Good-bye

It is easiest if an old dog passes away in his sleep. However, you might eventually be faced with the painful decision of whether or not to put your dog to sleep. Your veterinarian can help you assess the quality of your dog's life, especially if your dog is being treated for a fatal disease, such as an inoperable tumor. Your instincts might also help you know when your dog is not happy and his pain overrides his ability to enjoy life. You will be able to endure your grief more easily when you make the decision with love and care. Ask if your veterinarian is willing to come to your home for the procedure. The comfortable, familiar surroundings will make it easier for both you and your dog.

HOW-TO: GROOMING

Brushing

The Weimaraner's short glossy coat is easy to care for and does not require special brushing. A rubber brush or glove is ideal to help remove loose hair. A chamois leather cloth will give the coat a smooth shine. Mud is easily brushed off once it is dry.

All dogs shed, although compared to many breeds a Weimaraner's shedding is less noticeable. Their short fine hairs are like eyelashes and do not readily stick to clothes or furniture, but usually just fall to the floor. The gray color of the hairs is neutral and not readily seen, but the dogs will leave a fine dusting of hair if allowed on furniture. Weimaraners shed most obviously in the spring. Because they do not have a thick undercoat, molting is easily

Be very careful to avoid getting shampoo in your dog's eyes and ears.

dealt with by a quick brushing every few days.

Bathing

Because of their short coat, Weimaraners seldom need a bath and do not often smell pungent. Some collars retain a strong doggy smell and a new collar rather than a bath might be necessary. Otherwise, it is time for a bath if you pet your dog and your hands become coated with a film of dirt. Weimaraners love to swim but, like most dogs, they are not enamored of a bath, no matter how warm the water and how neutral-smelling the shampoo. Giving your dog an occasional bath while he is still young will get him used to the experience.

Most dogs dislike the slippery surface of a bathtub because it offers no traction. It is often easier to bathe your dog outside using a hose that attaches to your inside faucet.

✔ Use warm water.
✔ Be careful not to get shampoo in your dog's eyes or ears.
✔ Rinse thoroughly.
✔ Your dog can dry in the warm sun, but if it is cool outside, rub your dog dry with a towel and keep him inside.

Nails

The nails of most Weimaraners do not wear down by themselves and will need to be

trimmed. If you can hear your dog's nails click against a hard floor, or if the nails touch the floor surface, they are too long. Overgrown nails can snag and tear. A torn nail is not only painful; it can become infected. Markedly overgrown nails can cause a dog to walk incorrectly and even cause joint stress because the dog walks on the back half of his paws.

Cut the nails in front of the quick, which is the portion that contains the nails' blood supply and nerves. If your dog's nails are light-colored you can see the dark line of quick. Shining a flashlight at the nail will sometimes help to illuminate the quick.

Using a large nail trimmer made for dogs, snip off the portion in front of the quick. By trimming off small portions at a time rather than

The proper way to trim your dog's nails.

making one large cut, you are less likely to accidentally cut the quick. If you do draw blood, apply pressure with a wet cloth for three to five minutes to stop the bleeding. If you have questions about nail trimming, consult your veterinarian.

When teaching a puppy to allow his nails to be clipped, be slow and patient. Snip just a little off of each nail, or cut just one or two nails a day if necessary. Make it a low-key, positive experience.

Dental Care

Dogs can suffer from periodontal disease, abscesses, and tooth decay and loss. To prevent these conditions, a dog's teeth need regular care. Teeth covered with tartar and inflamed gums can cause more than bad breath; the bacteria can travel from infected teeth and gums to the dog's heart and kidneys, causing serious infection.

Bones and hard crunchy foods can help prevent tartar from accumulating on your dog's teeth. Even so, by the time your Weimaraner is three years old, his teeth will probably have some tartar. Brushing once a week with a soft toothbrush and dog toothpaste will help keep them free of plaque and tartar. Do not use human toothpaste.

You can remove tartar with a variety of other products, including tooth scalers and scrapers. Because it is difficult to clean at the gum line, a professional cleaning is eventually necessary. Heavy tartar buildup usually needs to be removed by a veterinarian while your dog is sedated. The results will help keep your dog's teeth strong and healthy and keep his breath from smelling foul. Depending on the dog, a professional cleaning might be needed once every six months or once every two years. Your veterinarian can recommend how often your dog's teeth should be professionally cleaned.

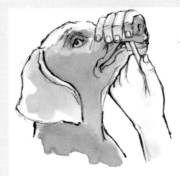

Brushing your dog's teeth.

Ear Care

Many Weimaraners seldom need to have their ears cleaned, but some individuals produce a lot of wax, or frequent dirty or dusty areas. Either way, you should make it a habit to check your dog's ears every week or so.

Keeping the ears clean of debris will help prevent them from becoming smelly and possibly infected. For many dogs, wiping the outer part clean with cotton balls will suffice. Carefully use a cotton swab to remove any wax or debris farther down the ear. Do not allow the swab to enter the ear canal, which is beyond the area you can easily see; doing so can seriously injure your dog's ear.

Ears that are continually dirty could indicate an infection or an infestation with ear mites, which are transmitted from other dogs. If your dog's ears smell bad, look irritated or have a discharge, he needs to be examined by a veterinarian.

Usually, if your dog gets something in his ear, such as a grass seed, he will shake or scratch at his head or carry his head at a tilt. Teaching your dog to allow you to examine his ears while he is still a puppy is useful, as you might be able to remove the offending object yourself. However, if you cannot see anything in your dog's ear, you must take him to a veterinarian.

FEEDING

What's in that Food?

Good nutrition is a key factor in promoting a long and healthy life for your dog. Dogs need a balanced and nutritious diet that includes the appropriate amounts of protein, carbohydrates, fats, vitamins, and minerals. Dog foods are made with a combination of meat and grain ingredients. A particular food product's ingredients are listed in descending order by weight. The first three to five items on an ingredient list make up most of the food.

On every bag or can of dog food is a guaranteed analysis, which tells you what amount of protein, fat, fiber, and moisture is in the food. The protein and fat contents are stated as minimums, while the fiber and moisture contents are stated as maximums. The word "crude," which precedes each measure, refers to laboratory analysis rather than digestibility.

The ingredients used to meet a dog's nutritional requirements can vary widely among different brands of dog food. Sources of protein include beef, lamb, and poultry (whole and by-products), milk, eggs, fish, meat, bone meal, corn, and soybeans. Protein is needed for the growth and maintenance of muscle and for the production of antibodies, hormones, and enzymes. Sources of carbohydrates include grains such as rice, corn, wheat, and soybeans. Carbohydrates perform numerous functions, such as providing energy.

A proper diet is crucial to your Weimaraner's continued good health.

Animal fat, such as poultry fat or beef tallow, is the usual source of fat in dog food. Fat is a concentrated source of energy that provides twice as many calories per serving as protein or carbohydrates. It is a necessary carrier for fat-soluble vitamins. As a source of essential fatty acids, fat helps provide your dog with a healthy coat and skin. The percent of linoleic acid, one of the essential fatty acids, is sometimes given in a product's guaranteed analysis. Linoleic acid in particular is associated with a lustrous coat and healthy skin. Most important from your dog's perspective, fat can enhance a food's palatability. The outside of many types of kibble is basted with fat so that it tastes better.

Types of Food

Commercial dog food is available in three forms: dry, canned, and semimoist. Nutritionally complete and balanced dry food is the most economical way to feed your dog. Because of its low moisture content, dry food is usually more concentrated, with more calories per gram than either canned or semimoist foods. Dry food is sold in a variety of sizes, from five to fifty pounds. To feed the freshest food, it is best to buy only one month's supply of food at a time. Dry food is the most popular type of dog food and comes in more varieties than either canned or semimoist. The hard, abrasive surface of dry food helps to decrease the accumulation of dental tartar on the teeth of some dogs. Dry food can be left in your dog's dish all day because it will not spoil. Keep in mind, however, that ants and other vermin might be attracted to the food.

Canned dog foods come in a variety of flavors, textures, and types. Compared to dry food, canned food is more expensive per pound. The moisture level of canned food is about 75 percent, compared to only about eight percent in dry foods and 30 percent in semimoist foods. To satisfy your dog's caloric and nutritional needs, he will need to eat more if his diet is composed only of canned food. Because of the cost and the amount of food needed, few people feed their dogs only canned food. You might notice that the percentage of crude protein and fat on the guaranteed analysis of canned food is much lower than that given for a dry food. However, when adjusted for the canned food's moisture content, the food will contain appropriate amounts of protein and fat. Most dogs find canned food more palatable than dry food. Canned food can spoil if left uneaten in your dog's dish.

Semimoist food is often made to look like hamburger and is usually available in several flavors. This type of food usually has obvious added food color. The shape and color are meant to appeal to people rather than to dogs. Semimoist foods have a high digestibility because one source of carbohydrates is sugars, which also provide antibacterial stability and help the food retain moisture. Semimoist food is more calorically dense than canned foods, but is not as concentrated as most dry foods. Many semimoist foods are designed only for adult dogs. Like dry food, semimoist foods are convenient to feed and can be left out all day.

Life Stage and Specialty Diets

A dog's nutritional requirements change as he grows from a puppy into an adult, and change again as he ages. Many dog food manufacturers have developed different types of foods to meet these changing nutritional needs. These life-stage foods are labeled for puppies, adults, and senior dogs. Other specialty diets are made for certain conditions and include high calorie foods for active and working dogs, sometimes called performance foods, and lower calorie foods for overweight dogs.

Life stage and specialty foods are more precisely formulated than those with a one-size-fits-all approach and usually incorporate the latest research findings. Feeding these types of foods can best meet your dog's nutritional needs and help keep your Weimaraner in top health and condition throughout his life.

Feed your puppy a premium-quality puppy food. Formulated for growing puppies, these foods contain more protein and fat than foods for adult dogs. In general, Weimaraner puppies can be fed the puppy food for their first year, and then changed to an adult food. Excessive amounts of protein can cause muscles and other soft tissue to develop more quickly than the dog's skeletal structure. Many experts believe this can predispose a dog to conditions such as hip dysplasia. This is a concern for very large breeds of dogs. Nonetheless, if your Weimaraner puppy is growing at what seems a fast rate, discuss with the breeder and your veterinarian the possibility of changing to an adult dog food sooner than at one year.

Once your Weimaraner is seven years old, he should be switched to one of the senior diets that are available. These foods are lower in protein, fat, and calories and are designed to meet the nutritional needs of older dogs. Because older dogs slow down and are less active, their calorie intake should be decreased. Your older Weimaraner will do better and be more energetic if he is not overweight. Obese dogs have a higher risk for heart disease, and excess weight puts more strain on their aging joints.

It is always easier to prevent your dog from becoming overweight than it is to put him on a reducing diet. While reduced calorie foods are available for overweight dogs, a dog that is obese also needs more exercise, not just a different food or less of his regular food. Canned food, with its higher moisture content, is an option for the overweight dog. Raw carrots are a low-calorie snack that can satisfy your dog's hunger. A beautiful animal such as the Weimaraner should look fit and gorgeous, whether a show dog or a pet. Because their smooth, sleek coat does not obscure their physique, an overweight Weimaraner can look like a dumpling. Weimaraners are an active breed and do not tend to gain weight unless improperly fed.

What to Feed

A large selection of commercial dog foods are available. Almost all of the brands sold in the United States provide an adequate diet according to the Association of American Feed Control Officers (AAFCO), which is an advisory body involved in the pet food industry. The AAFCO has nutrient profiles and standards that establish maximum and minimum nutrient requirements for dogs. The latter is important, because an excess of a nutrient can be just as bad as a nutritional deficiency. Foods that meet AAFCO standards state on their package that the food provides complete and balanced

nutrition for either all life stages (growth, reproduction, lactation, and adult dogs who are not pregnant), or for one or more life stages, such as growth and maintenance of dogs. It is unwise to buy and feed a food that does not contain such a statement.

Nonetheless, there is variation in the quality of commercial dog foods that do meet AAFCO standards. The adage "You get what you pay for" applies to dog food. Premium foods, which are the most expensive, tend to be superior and are recommended for your Weimaraner. These foods are more than just adequate. They usually have higher protein and fat content compared to generic, private label, and grocery store brands. The ingredients that make up premium products are typically more expensive, such as higher-quality animal protein (lamb meal compared to meat and bone meal) and natural preservatives, such as vitamins C and E. (To prevent the fat in dry foods from spoiling, some type of preservative is necessary.) The first ingredient in premium foods is usually an animal-based protein such as chicken, rather than a plant-based protein such as corn. Premium foods do not usually come in fancy shapes and color.

Because the higher-quality ingredients in a premium food are more digestible and nourishing per serving, your dog will not need to eat as much as a food with poorer-quality sources of nutrients. Dogs fed foods based primarily on grains, such as ground corn, usually need to eat more per pound of body weight and, consequently, produce a larger stool.

Obviously, many dogs do well enough on foods that are not premium, or else the foods would not still be sold. However, dogs who are fed premium foods appear healthier, with more lustrous coats, better skin condition, and fewer

digestive problems. Premium dog foods are sold at pet stores, veterinarian offices, and feed stores. A few brands are sold at grocery stores.

Tip: The main criteria you should use to select a food is your dog's response to it.
✔ How does your dog look?
✔ Is his fur dry or glossy?
✔ Is his skin flaky?
✔ Does he constantly scratch himself even if he has no fleas?
✔ Does he have a good appetite?

People often switch brands when their dog's coat does not look shiny or their dog's skin is dry. If you change your dog's food, you should do so over a period of a week, gradually mixing the new food with the old. While some dogs can tolerate an abrupt change, others will experience a digestive upset, such as diarrhea.

A high-quality kibble is the most practical way to feed your Weimaraner. Dogs do not

Puppies need to eat more food for their size than do adults.

need variety and do perfectly well on one brand of dog food all their life. However, there is no good reason not to provide your dog with some nutritionally balanced variety. Dogs do show enthusiasm for the addition of some canned or semimoist food with their regular kibble.

How Much to Feed

The feeding instructions on a bag or a can of dog food are general recommendations, usually based on a dog's weight. Consider the instructions a starting point. Your dog might need to eat slightly more or less. The proper portion to feed your dog is whatever amount is necessary to maintain his optimum weight and condition.

If necessary, your veterinarian can help you determine your dog's ideal weight. In between periodically weighing him, you can still tell if your dog is receiving the right amount of food. You should not be able to easily see your dog's ribs, but you should be able to easily feel them and his backbone through a slight layer of muscle and fat.

The amount of food your dog will need to eat is affected by numerous factors. Just as individual people vary in their metabolism, and how much food they can eat without gaining weight, so do individual dogs. Even dogs who live in the same household and are related may have as much as a two-fold difference in the amount of food needed to maintain their weight.

Naturally, active dogs need more food than less active dogs. Weimaraners used for hunting

Consult with your veterinarian on the optimal feeding program to help your dog reach his potential.

can consume up to 40 percent more food during the hunting season than they normally do. Competitive events, such as tracking, can also increase a dog's appetite. Your dog might need more food if he regularly accompanies you on bike rides, hikes, or runs.

If such activities decrease or stop, you should lessen the amount of food you feed your dog if he starts to gain weight. Sedentary dogs require about 20 percent less food than active dogs. A Weimaraner who needs to be kept quiet and inactive—for example, one with a cast on a broken leg—might need to have his regular ration slightly decreased to prevent weight gain. Your veterinarian can provide such a recommendation.

The weather can affect how much food your dog eats. Just as people's appetites increase during cold weather, so might your dog's. Researchers know that dogs eat about 3.5 percent more food for every 1.8°F increase in wind-chill factor below 59°F (15°C). If you take your dog for a long cross-country ski in snowy

weather, you might observe that he has a ravenous appetite upon your return home. Just as people prefer light food during hot summer weather, you might notice that your dog's appetite decreases somewhat. On average, dogs eat about 1 percent to 1.5 percent less food for each 1.8°F rise in ambient temperature above 77°F (25°C).

Compared to unaltered dogs, "fixed" dogs often have a slower metabolism. Many dogs are altered shortly before or after they reach puberty, a time when their growth has slowed anyway, and they do not need to eat as much food as when they were growing puppies. Once your dog is spayed or neutered, carefully monitor your pet's weight to determine whether you need to adjust the amount of food you feed. Besides your being able to feel his ribs, your Weimaraner should have a waist.

Most Weimaraners have hearty appetites. Some could eat until they are stuffed and still want more; a few are picky and eat only what they need, no matter how much food is provided. You will learn which type your dog is. If your dog does not eat his food, he might not be hungry. Try offering his meal at a later time. However, if your dog loses his appetite, especially for several days, he might be sick and should be taken to a veterinarian.

When to Feed

The breeder from whom you purchased your Weimaraner puppy probably gave you a recommended feeding schedule. Weimaraner puppies between two and three months old are fed three or four equal-sized meals a day. Feed only two or three meals a day after your puppy is three months old. If necessary, you can soften the dry food with warm water to make it easier for your puppy to eat. Puppies older than five months should be fed twice a day, once in the morning and once in the evening. Ideally, you should feed your puppy his meals at the same time every day. This will help you housebreak him, because puppies eliminate shortly after eating. After every meal you should take your puppy outside to do his business.

Scheduled mealtimes will work only if you are home during the day. If you work during the day, the alternative method is to free-feed your puppy. Free-fed puppies have access to dry food at all times.

Puppies that are free-fed rarely overeat and become fat. A growing puppy should have a shiny coat and his ribs should show slightly.

Adult Weimaraners should have two meals a day. You might opt to give your dog a few large dog biscuits in the morning and a full-size meal at night. Because Weimaraners are potentially subject to bloat, an emergency medical condition described in detail in the health section, it is important not to feed your dog a large meal and then take him out to exercise right away.

Some dogs prefer to eat their meal in a quiet part of the house; others are not bothered by a

There are a number of different food-dish styles to choose from.

lot of activity. Some dogs become protective of their food dish and the area in which they are fed. It is unacceptable for a dog to growl or lunge at an adult or child who walks by or up to the dog while he is eating. Weimaraners are very people-oriented dogs and rarely exhibit such tendencies. Nonetheless, you should teach your Weimaraner manners at his mealtime. Your dog should "sit" and "stay" for his meal, and eat only when released. Consult a dog trainer if your puppy or adult dog shows aggressive behavior when fed.

Drinking Water

Make sure your Weimaraner always has clean, fresh water. If your dog spends time both indoors and out, he should have water bowls in both locations. If needed, heated water bowls, which prevent water from freezing, are sold for outside use. A Lixit (sold in pet stores) can be attached to an outside faucet to provide a constant supply of clean drinking water.

Note: Water bowls need to be washed at least every few days. A slime can coat the bowls, which will not be removed by simply emptying and refilling with water.

Food and Water Dishes

A plethora of dog dishes are available, including stainless steel, heavy-duty ceramic, and lightweight plastic. Whatever type you choose, it is most important that the dish be easy for you to wash and clean. Some manufacturers now make stands in which to place your dog's food and water dishes. The stands

are supposed to make it more comfortable for your pet to eat and relieve strain on his back and neck.

Supplements, Table Scraps, and Treats

Nutritionally complete premium foods provide the necessary amounts of vitamins, minerals, and trace elements. Dietary supplements are not usually needed and can actually cause problems from oversupplementation. However, foods of lesser quality might need to be supplemented. Your veterinarian can instruct you if doing so is necessary.

A word of advice: Keep in mind that the added cost of the supplement might make it cost-effective to buy a higher-quality food.

When it comes to feeding dogs, opinions are as numerous as the stars overhead. Many people are adamantly against feeding a dog any kind of human food. Others enjoy sharing table scraps with their dog. As long as table scraps do not comprise more than 10 percent of your dog's diet, they are unlikely to cause any problems. However, when table scraps regularly comprise more than 25 percent of your dog's diet, problems such as obesity and imbalanced nutrition can occur. Never feed your dog bones from your leftover meals. Suitable bones are discussed in the section on toys.

Caution: Dogs like sweets such as chocolate. However, chocolate contains theobromine, which is toxic to dogs, and can cause urinary incontinence, seizures, and death. Do not feed your dog chocolate and be sure to keep any out of your clever Weimaraner's reach.

COMMON AILMENTS AND MEDICAL PROBLEMS

Pet Health Insurance

Veterinary medicine is becoming more sophisticated and also more costly. In cases of catastrophic illness or accident, pet health insurance can come to the rescue for owners who might otherwise have to put down their dog because they could not afford his medical treatment. Like health insurance for people, pet insurance is based on a dog's age, has waiting periods for policies to take effect, deductibles, payout limits per incident, and exclusions. Policies might not cover congenital, hereditary illnesses, or preexisting conditions, and might provide extremely limited coverage for older dogs. Ask your veterinarian for suggestions on a plan. Be sure to research your options before selecting a plan.

External Parasites

Mange Mites

Sarcoptic mange is caused by a mite that burrows into the dog's skin, causing severe itchiness and thickened skin. Demodectic mange is caused by a mite that is normally present in small numbers in the hair follicles of most healthy dogs. (The mites are not visible to the naked eye.) Typical signs are patches of hair loss, reddening of

Your puppy should be examined by a veterinarian within a few days of arriving at your home.

the skin, and scaling. It is most common in dogs younger than two years of age. Demodectic mange is thought to be associated with a depression of the dog's immune system from causes such as illness or shipping. A veterinarian can prescribe effective treatment after diagnosing mange mites from skin scrapings.

Fleas

Fleas are a year-round problem in some parts of the country. In other regions they are a concern only during the warmer part of the year. Fleas do not typically occur above 5,000 feet in elevation. Dogs can get fleas from other dogs, cats, and wild animals. Areas where numerous dogs play, such as dog parks, can also be sources.

Some dogs are highly allergic to fleas, a condition called fleabite allergy. A flea injects saliva when it bites the dog, which causes skin irritation and scratching. Heavy infestations can cause anemia and fleas are also vectors for tapeworms. You are also likely to get bitten.

The life cycle of the flea includes egg, larva, pupa, and adult and takes place both on and off your dog. The adult flea drinks your dog's blood. Most flea eggs are found on the floor and locations where the dog sleeps, such as his bed. Within a few days, the eggs hatch into larvae. The larvae eat adult flea droppings, which are full of blood. Several weeks after hatching, the larvae pupate, and then hatch into the adult. This transformation can take from a week to as long as a year.

It can be difficult to eliminate fleas, but it is possible to control them. Flea powders, sprays, shampoos, and collars are options, but by themselves will not get rid of all fleas. Unfortunately, herbal remedies such as garlic and brewer's yeast are not typically effective against fleas.

Caution: Flea collars can cause toxic reactions in some dogs and should not be used on puppies.

Breaking the lifecycle is an effective means to control fleas. Many flea products kill the adults, but the eggs, larvae, and pupa still survive in your dog's environment. Products prescribed by your veterinarian can prevent the larvae and pupa from transforming into adult fleas.

Using flea control products on your dog, and some type of insecticide inside and outside your house is most effective. Products are available from pet stores and veterinary clinics for this

female   male
**Black-legged tick
or Deer tick**

female   male
**Adult brown
dog tick**

**Adult relapsing
fever tick**

female   male
Lone star tick

female   male
**American dog
tick**

purpose, or a commercial pest control service can be used. Using a combination of methods (not products) is a good strategy. Vacuum your house, especially where you dog spends his time, and wash your dog's bedding at least once a week.

In their frustration, some people overuse flea products. Combining different products is potentially hazardous because of toxicity that could produce an adverse reaction in your dog. Consult with your veterinarian for the best methods to use for your situation. Treatment of a heavy infestation of fleas is best done under your veterinarian's guidance and might require the services of a pest control company. Besides your dog, any pet cats must also be treated.

Flea combs are very effective on the Weimaraner's short coat. The fleas get trapped in the fine teeth of the comb and can then be killed with your fingers or washed into a cup of water with bleach or detergent. The narrow teeth also catch the flea dirt, thus removing a source of food for the flea larvae. Using a flea comb can help you monitor the success of your flea control efforts. Combing your dog for a few minutes every day is an effective way of giving your dog some immediate relief from biting fleas.

Ticks

Ticks are active mainly in spring and summer. Depending on their geographic range, they can carry a variety of diseases, including Lyme disease and Rocky Mountain Spotted Fever.

When taking your dog into areas with ticks, temporarily using a flea and tick collar can help reduce the number of ticks that climb onto your dog. Before you get into the car, or as soon as you get home, examine your dog for

Ticks come in a variety of shapes and sizes.

ticks. A flea comb is useful for finding ticks, but be careful not to rip out a tick imbedded in your dog. If the tick's mouthparts are left behind, they can cause an infection.

If you find a tick biting your dog, do not remove it with your bare hands. The spirochete that causes Lyme disease can enter through your skin. Apply alcohol to the tick with a cotton-tipped applicator. The tick will be dead in a few minutes. Using tweezers, grasp the tick as close to the skin as possible and pull steadily to remove it. Dispose of the tick by flushing it down the toilet.

A vaccination for Lyme disease is available. However, veterinarians typically recommend it only if there is a high incidence of Lyme disease in your area or if your dog's activities, such as hunting, put him at risk. Your veterinarian can advise you whether your Weimaraner should be vaccinated.

Internal Parasites

Roundworms, hookworms, tapeworms, and heartworms are the most common internal parasites that affect dogs. If undetected and left untreated, internal parasites can be a serious problem. Part of a new puppy checkup entails bringing a stool sample that is checked for the eggs of internal parasites. Your veterinarian will recommend whether annual checks are necessary. For all cases of internal parasites, rely on your veterinarian to diagnose and treat the condition with a deworming medication.

Roundworms

Roundworms inhabit the gastrointestinal tract of dogs. This common parasite can infest unborn puppies in their mother's womb or through their mother's milk when nursing. Although roundworms seldom cause symptoms in adult dogs, symptoms in puppies are generally more severe. A puppy infected with roundworms has a potbelly, a rough, dull coat, and looks thin because he has poor muscle development. Common symptoms include vomiting and diarrhea, and sometimes the adult worms are vomited or eliminated in the feces.

Hookworms

Several species of hookworms can inhabit the dog's small intestines. Hookworms are more common in warm, humid climates than in arid regions. In the environment, hookworm eggs hatch into free-living larvae with a short life span. While the eggs or larvae of other internal parasites can survive for years until they enter a dog host, the hookworm larvae can only live about two months. Depending on the species, hookworms can be transmitted via a dam's

The proper way to administer a pill: place it in the back of the dog's mouth.

milk, through the skin, or by swallowing the larvae. Anemia is the main symptom of infection. Hookworms can sometimes be difficult to eradicate because they survive in other parts of a dog's body, where their development is arrested. When a dewormer kills the worms in a dog's intestines, the worms in other parts of the dog's body become active. Adult dogs often develop an immune response that kills the worms before they reach maturity.

Tapeworms

Several species of tapeworms can infest dogs. Tapeworms use intermediate hosts, such as fleas and rodents, to facilitate transmission to dogs and other mammals. The most common species is transmitted by fleas. Tapeworms can be a common internal parasite when a dog has fleas.

A dog becomes infested while grooming when he swallows a flea containing tapeworm larvae.

Infested dogs might scoot along the floor, or occasionally, the white ricelike tapeworm segments can be observed crawling on the dog's hind end, his bedding, or droppings. In addition to deworming, flea control measures are essential to protect your dog against future infestation by tapeworms.

Heartworms

Heartworms are transmitted from dog to dog by the bite of an infected mosquito. The mosquito swallows the larval heartworms when it

The best way to deal with internal parasites like heartworms is to prevent them from affecting your dog at all.

A regular vaccination schedule will help keep your dog strong and healthy, with shiny coats like these two Weimaraners.

bites an infested dog. The larvae are passed into another dog when the mosquito feasts again. The larvae develop in subcutaneous tissues. Then, they travel to their final destination—the dog's heart.

Note: Heartworms are dangerous because they can kill a dog.

Heartworm infection can be avoided with the use of preventive medication. The medication is easy to administer because dogs like the chewable tablet and the tablet needs to be given only once a month. Before starting the medication, a veterinarian will take a blood sample to be sure your dog is not already infected.

In some parts of the country, mosquitoes are active all year and a dog should be given heartworm preventive medication throughout the year. In other areas, mosquitoes are present for only a few months. A dog might need to be on the medication for only as long as mosquitoes are active. If your dog goes off the preventive medication, some veterinarians prefer to retest before starting the medication again. If you travel to a region of the country where heartworms are present, ask your veterinarian about starting the treatment before and while you are visiting.

Immunizations

Vaccines are given to prevent your dog from getting infectious diseases. Vaccinations are necessary because no specific treatments exist

Giving your dog a quick rub on a regular basis will help you look for unusual lumps or bumps.

vaccination should be given routinely to dogs that come in contact with other dogs at boarding kennels, shows, and dog parks.

Between three to four months of age, your puppy is given his first rabies vaccine. A second rabies vaccine is given when the young dog is between twelve and fifteen months of age. Different states have different requirements for revaccinations, from every year to every three years.

Changing Vaccine Protocols

Some Weimaraner breeders use and recommend what is called the Weimaraner or special immunization schedule, whose components include administering only killed canine parvovirus vaccine and not using combination vaccines. Ideally, before you pick up your puppy, the breeder will alert you to this need. Breeders who use this schedule also recommend waiting as long as possible to give the rabies vaccine (up to one year) after the initial vaccines are given.

Your veterinarian might need to special-order the vaccines. Many veterinary hospitals have combination vaccines (called 5, 6, and 7 in 1 modified live vaccines), not the single vaccine products. A breeder who recommends that you follow the special immunization schedule might not guarantee your puppy if you fail to follow his recommendation. If your veterinarian is unwilling to comply with the breeder's vaccination schedule, find another veterinarian who will.

Some breeders use the single-vaccine schedule because puppies get sick after receiving the

to fight these pathogens (such as parvovirus) once a dog is infected. The risk of these diseases has been effectively reduced by the widespread use of vaccination programs. For the first few weeks of your puppy's life, the antibodies present in the colostrum (first milk) from the mother will protect the puppy. However, if the mother has not developed immunity, neither will the puppy.

For protection against numerous infectious diseases, puppies are typically immunized against distemper, hepatitis, parvovirus, parainfluenza, coronavirus, and leptospirosis. Referred to as the puppy series, the shots are usually administered over a period of two to four months. Your puppy's first inoculation might have already been administered by the breeder, or it might need to be given by your veterinarian. After the series is complete, an adult dog receives an annual vaccine booster for these same diseases.

Bordetella is also called kennel cough. It is a highly contagious disease, with symptoms that include coughing, sneezing, hacking, and retching. It can last for several days to several weeks. A vaccine is available but does not protect against all strains of this condition. The combination vaccines and because of concerns about the combination vaccines triggering immune-mediated disorders (see hypertrophic osteodystrophy, page 82). Some lines of Weimaraners seem disposed to adverse reactions from the combination vaccines, which can occur one to two days after inoculation, though symptoms might be delayed for ten to thirty days. Typical signs of an immune reaction include fever, stiffness, and sore joints. In an effort to reduce this risk, the alternative protocol was developed by veterinarian researchers.

In addition, instead of yearly vaccination, annual blood tests (called titres) that measure the dog's level of immunity are performed for dogs that previously experienced an adverse reaction to vaccination, or are at genetic or physiological risk for reactions. If the level of immunity to infectious agents is too low, the dog is given the necessary vaccination. As more is learned, these vaccine protocols might further change.

Note: The Internet site for the Weimaraner Club of America is a good source of information for any future recommendations.

Other Conditions

Dogs do not get colds. If your dog has symptoms indicative of a cold, such as runny eyes and nose, something is wrong and he should be seen by a veterinarian. Other symptoms indicating the need for a visit to the veterinarian include long bouts of vomiting, diarrhea, or constipation. Loss of appetite is also an indication that something is amiss. Like all purebred dogs, the Weimaraner is subject to certain other ailments and conditions, which are discussed in the rest of this chapter.

Bloat

Bloat, also called gastric dilatation-volvulus (GDV), is a serious, life-threatening condition that can affect Weimaraners and other deep-chested, large and giant breed dogs. The exact causes of this condition are not known. However, it usually occurs when a dog overeats, bolts food, swallows air, drinks large amounts of water immediately after eating, exercises vigorously before or after meals, and/or when stressful situations cause the dog to become agitated. Air and fluid accumulate in the stomach that the dog cannot relieve by burping or vomiting.

Signs of bloat include abdominal enlargement, which looks like swelling just past your dog's rib cage, excessive salivation, attempting to vomit without being able to do so, and abdominal tenderness. At first a dog might be restless, but he will eventually become lethargic. In severe cases, the bloated stomach might pouch out on one side of the dog's abdomen. The condition rapidly progresses and an affected dog will exhibit signs of shock, such as pale gums, weakness, and increased heart and respiration rate. Any of these symptoms indicates that you should immediately take your dog to the veterinarian for emergency treatment.

Unless immediately treated by a veterinarian, the dog could die. A veterinarian will take X rays to determine whether the stomach has rotated. Treatment consists of passing a tube into the stomach to remove the air and fluid; if the stomach has rotated, surgery is necessary. During surgery, some veterinarians will anchor the dog's stomach in place to help prevent the disease from recurring. Even when the treatment is successful, death can occur up to a week later because of shock or complications.

Bloat is expensive to treat and can be fatal even with veterinary treatment; prevention is

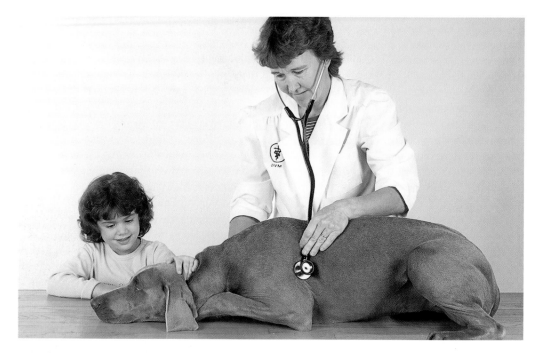

Ideally, your Weimaraner will grow comfortable with his veterinarian over the years.

best. Instead of one large meal, feed two meals a day, one in the morning and one in the evening. Limit the dog's exercise for two hours before and after he eats. The Internet site of the Weimaraner Club of America is a good source of information as more is learned about the causes and prevention of this ailment.

Hip Dysplasia

Hip dysplasia is a hereditary disease that can affect Weimaraners. In affected dogs, the ball-and-socket joint of one or both hips develop abnormally, which allows the "ball" end of the

Weimaraners are very active dogs.

thighbone to separate from the hip joint. This causes degeneration and erosion of the joint cartilage and bony surfaces. This condition can be painful, cause lameness, and reduce levels of activity. Rapid growth, overfeeding, and excessive exercise can influence the severity of the disease.

Hip dysplasia can suddenly appear in a young dog, or it may gradually appear as the dog matures. The condition is diagnosed by X rays of the hip joints. Treatment of hip dysplasia can involve moderate daily exercise to help strengthen the underlying muscles and

Right: A handsome Weimaraner "smiles" for the camera.

Bottom: Weimaraners typically love to swim.

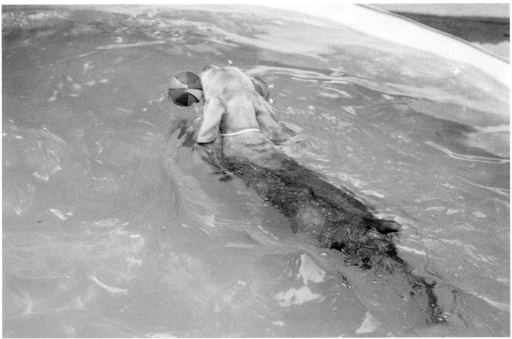

tendons supporting the affected joint; anti-inflammatory medications to help relieve pain; and surgery, either to clean and rebuild the joints to help reduce pain and improve function or to perform total hip replacement.

The Orthopedic Foundation for Animals (OFA) has established guidelines for testing and detecting hip dysplasia in dogs two years old or older. The OFA reviews X rays of a dog's hips. If the X rays show no evidence of the condition, the OFA will certify that the dog is free of the condition. It is highly recommended that all dogs used for breeding have their hips x-rayed and rated by the OFA at age two, before being bred.

Hypertrophic Osteodystrophy

Hypertrophic osteodystrophy (HOD) occurs in rapidly growing large breeds and usually affects puppies between three and seven months of age. An abnormal inflammation of the growth plates of the bones occurs, which can be detected with X rays. Symptoms include pain, lameness, lethargy, reluctance to move or stand, and sometimes an elevated temperature and loss of appetite. In Weimaraners, this condition is often associated with an autoimmune reaction that occurs in response to the administration of combination vaccinations. The disease usually lasts for two to three weeks and is sometimes followed by less severe recurrences. Treatment is variable, but often includes large doses of steroids, aspirin, and antibiotics.

Hypothyroidism

Hypothyroidism is a common hormonal disease caused by a deficiency of thyroid hormone. Decreased thyroid function usually occurs when the thyroid gland is destroyed. Causes of damage include immune-mediated inflammation of the thyroid gland or cancer. Sometimes the condition is congenital (existing since birth). Symptoms include a reluctance to exercise, mental lethargy, weight gain (without an increase in appetite or food intake), and a dull, dry coat. Other signs include dark pigmentation of the skin, hair loss, and scaly skin. These symptoms are often gradual in appearance. A Weimaraner with hypothyroidism is treated with synthetic thyroid pills, usually given twice a day. The medication must be continued throughout the dog's life. Once treatment has begun, the improvement in the dog's appearance and attitude is marked.

Skin Problems

Weimaraners sometimes develop hot spots, which are a self-induced, traumatic skin injury. Lesions on the skin result from licking, chewing, and scratching; the spots are secondarily affected by bacteria. Hot spots occur on the thighs and lower back above the tail. Lick granuloma is another skin condition Weimaraners can develop. It is caused when a dog obsessively licks an area of skin, usually on the feet. The affected area is often oval and hairless. Boredom is the usual cause of this condition, which can be difficult to cure. Treatment usually entails changing the dog's daily routine, application of a bitter-tasting substance on the skin (e.g., Bitter Apple), or an Elizabethan collar, which prevents the dog from licking himself. Your veterinarian can diagnose and treat these conditions.

Weimaraners sometimes get *Staphylococcus* bacteria infections on their skin. Because the

Not all lumps are necessarily cancerous, but if you find one be sure to seek veterinary care immediately.

symptoms are similar to flea allergy, the condition can be misdiagnosed. A skin scraping can help your veterinarian determine the cause of the skin problem and prescribe the appropriate treatment.

Food allergies can also cause skin problems. Often foods based on corn or wheat must be avoided. Your veterinarian can help you determine to what foods, if any, your dog is allergic.

Because their skin is thin and not protected with a thick coat of fur, Weimaraners can get scraped and cut when running in fields and forests. This is one reason competitors choose first to earn their dog's show championship, and then compete in field trials where the presence of cuts or scars is less of a problem. Minor cuts and tears can be treated at home by washing and cleaning the wound. However, wounds from barbed wire, puncture wounds due to dog fights, and bleeding cuts on the feet must be treated by a veterinarian.

dog is very old, your veterinarian might recommend waiting, because surgery has its own risks. In addition, the malignancies might recur.

Weimaraners can get sebaceous cysts, which look like a marble under the skin. Unless the cyst attaches to a muscle, grows, or causes your dog discomfort, many veterinarians recommend that it not be removed. Mammary tumors, which are easily seen around the teats, sometimes develop in older bitches.

Lumps and Bumps

Because the Weimaraner has a short, smooth coat, lumps and bumps are easily detected by a pet owner. Not all lumps are cancerous. However, your veterinarian should examine any lump and might take a biopsy to determine whether the growth is malignant. Weimaraners are known to develop benign or malignant tumors from mast cells, which are a specialized component of the skin. Cancerous growths can be surgically removed, but if they are slow-growing, do not cause the dog any discomfort, and the

Snake Bite

A poisonous snake's bite must be treated by a veterinarian, preferably with the appropriate antivenin. Keep your dog quiet and immobilized on the trip to the vet. Ice packs and a tourniquet are temporary measures that can slow the spread of the venom. Poisonous snakes are found throughout the continental United States. Because hunting dogs are at risk, gun dog clubs often sponsor rattlesnake aversion clinics that teach dogs to avoid being bitten.

GROUP
SECOND
SANTA BARBARA
KENNEL CLUB
JULY
97
BERGMAN PHOTOS

SHARING YOUR LIFE WITH A WEIMARANER

The Weimaraner is a versatile breed capable of participating in a variety of enjoyable activities. A closeness and rapport develop between an owner and Weimaraner when they share activities they both love. Working with your dog so that he learns new skills and watching him perform are rewarding. You will be proud of your dog, especially when he performs well enough to be awarded notice in competitive events.

Organized competitions and events are a great way for you and your dog to have fun while working together as a team, to get some exercise, and to meet other dog enthusiasts. The AKC publishes the *Gazette*, which is the official journal for the sport of purebred dogs. The events section within the *Gazette* lists upcoming shows and events and gives information on how to register.

Field Trials

Field trials test a dog's ability to perform the functions of his breed. The AKC field trials are highly competitive events in which dogs compete against each other for various titles. The dogs compete in various stakes, such as puppy, derby, gun dog, and open all age. Points

Dog shows can be very exciting for both you and your dog.

awarded for first place accumulate toward the title of Field Champion or Amateur Field Champion. Handling is usually done from horseback unless the dog is entered in a "walking stake."

The Weimaraner competes in AKC field trials for the pointing breeds. These trials test the ability of the dog to scent game (such as planted pheasant or quail), to go on point, and to remain staunch on point. Dogs competing in field trials must be in top condition and able to withstand the rigorous competitive conditions.

The North American Versatile Hunting Dog Association (NAVHDA) also sponsors hunting tests (see page 92 for address). The NAVHDA tests are designed to evaluate a dog's hereditary hunting characteristics and the trained dog's usefulness to the on-foot hunter in both field and water, before and after the shot, and as a finished hunting companion. Compared to field trials, the NAVHDA tests most closely simulate natural hunting conditions. The titles that can be earned are Natural Ability Test (NA), Utility Preparatory Test (UPT), and the Utility Test (UT). The tests are progressively more difficult. Rather than a comparative performance, NAVHDA judges evaluate a dog by a standard of performance, with a minimum performance in every area. The NAVHDA tests are similar to those used in Germany to evaluate the hunting Weimaraner.

AKC Hunting Tests

Hunting tests are noncompetitive events sanctioned by the AKC. The events are organized and run by local specialty clubs. The hunting test titles that can be earned are Junior Hunter (JH), Senior Hunter (SH), and Master Hunter (MH). Hunting tests are more casual than field trials. The dogs are handled on foot. Instead of competing against other dogs, each dog's hunting ability is judged against established hunting standards. The dogs are rated on hunting, trainability, bird-finding ability, and pointing. The SH and MH are also rated on retrieving. Hunting tests are more relaxed affairs than field trials and are good occasions to socialize with fellow hunters and bird dog enthusiasts.

Weimaraner Club of America Shooting and Retrieving Ratings

The Weimaraner Club of America sponsors rating tests that document a dog's hunting and retrieving ability. The two rating tests have three levels of increasing difficulty. A dog is scored pass or fail. The dogs may be handled either on foot or from horseback. The titles that can be earned include Novice Shooting Dog (NSD), Shooting Dog (SD), Shooting Dog Excellent (SDX), Novice Retrieving Dog (NRD), Retrieving Dog (RD), and Retrieving Dog Excellent (RDX). These tests assess a dog's natural hunting aptitude, style, hunting range, ability to locate game, and so forth. Because they are classified as a pointing breed, Weimaraners are not allowed to enter AKC retrieving trials. However, the WCA ratings evaluate this important skill.

Obedience Trials and Titles

Obedience trials are competitive events where dogs perform a specific group of exercises on command. The dogs start with a perfect score of 200 and judges deduct points for various violations, such as slowness or lack of attention. Dogs who do well in obedience competitions obey consistently, enjoy working with their owners, and are responsive to their owners' commands. A dog performs the obedience trial exercises off leash. Once your dog knows

═══ CHECKLIST ═══

The CGC Test

Your trainer can help you prepare for the CGC test. Local dog clubs usually offer the pass/fail test several times a year. Dogs who pass are awarded a Canine Good Citizenship Certificate. Proof of rabies vaccination is required to participate. The CGC test rates dogs in the following areas:

✔ Willingness to accept the approach of a friendly stranger.
✔ Sitting politely for petting.
✔ Walking on a loose leash.
✔ Walking through a crowd.
✔ Appearance and grooming.
✔ Reaction to another dog.
✔ Reaction to distraction.
✔ *Sit* and *down* on command and *staying* in place.
✔ Behavior when left alone, supervised separation.
✔ *Come* when called.

basic obedience commands both on and off leash, you can enter obedience trials and work toward earning your dog's first degree, CD, Companion Dog. The obedience titles that can be earned are Companion Dog (CD), which is earned in Novice Class; Companion Dog Excellent (CDX), which is earned in Open Class; and Utility Dog (UD), which is earned in Utility Class. The titles must be earned in sequence and each level is more competitive and difficult.

A trial is AKC licensed and points can be earned toward a title. A fun or sanctioned match is usually AKC approved, but is only for fun and practice. A copy of the official Obedience Regulations can be obtained from the AKC (see page 92).

Canine Good Citizenship

The AKC sponsors the Canine Good Citizenship (CGC) test to encourage dog owners to train their dogs. It is a good test of the skills and behavior that every dog should exhibit. The test does not require the precision of obedience trials, where the dogs move with their owners like dance partners in a competition. Besides demonstrating that your dog is well behaved and socialized, passing the test can have practical purposes. People whose dogs pass the test use the CGC as a reference for landlords when renting a home.

Showing Your Weimaraner

Many people enjoy competing with their Weimaraner in conformation shows. The AKC sanctions all-breed shows in which multiple breeds compete. The Weimaraner Club of America sponsors specialty shows, which are held by regional clubs. Dogs compete in various classes such as Puppy Novice, Bred-by-Exhibitor, American-bred, and Open. Males compete against males and females against females, until the selection of the Best of Breed or Best in Show winner, which can be either female or male. Judges assess how closely the dogs conform to the ideal breed standard of temperament and physical characteristics. The winners in each class are chosen by the process of elimination. The best show dogs enjoy what they are doing and like being in the show ring.

To earn a championship, a dog must accumulate 15 points at shows.

The points accumulated toward a championship must include wins from three different judges and at least two majors from different judges. Wins of three points or more are called a major win. The number of points earned at each show depends on how many dogs were entered for that breed. In every show, only one female and one male Weimaraner get the points. Finishing a dog's championship takes a lot of time and money. Dogs who do not finish their championships but have points toward a championship are called "pointed."

Dogs who enter shows cannot be spayed or neutered. Part of the purpose of shows is to identify dogs that are the best examples of their breed. These recognized individuals are then bred to produce puppies with the most desirable characteristics.

Junior Showmanship is an enjoyable activity for youngsters. Classes are divided by the child's age and sometimes by gender. Although the dog's grooming and overall condition are considered, a Junior Handler is not judged on the dog's conformation. Instead, the Junior

Handler is judged only on his or her ability and skill in presenting the dog.

A dog show judge evaluating how closely this Weimaraner fits the Breed Standard.

Therapy Dogs

Many Weimaraners are used as animal-assisted activity (AAA) and animal-assisted therapy (AAT) dogs. These dogs and their volunteer owners visit a variety of facilities, including nursing homes, hospitals, home healthcare, and hospices, and even team with physical therapists.

People who like people, together with sociable animals who like people, make the best teams. The Weimaraner's love of people, clever nature, and attractive looks help to make it an ideal candidate for this activity. The breed is easy for people to pet, because it is large enough to sit next to beds and wheelchairs. A good therapy dog is neither shy nor unruly. Weimaraners who are obedience trained and well mannered are best. The therapy dog should enjoy meeting people, but must not be pushy. The dog must have current vaccinations, be free of fleas, and clean for each visit.

Because Weimaraners often enjoy performing, some handlers teach their Weimaraners amusing tricks. For example, when the handler sneezes, the dog will pull a handkerchief out of the handler's pocket and give it to him.

Weimaraners are very skilled trackers.

A healthy Weimaraner's short coat is glossy.

A hunting dog requires more training than one kept as a pet.

Although tricks are not necessary for therapy work, any Weimaraner with a learning aptitude can be taught a variety of tricks, which are often appreciated by the people the team visits.

Trained evaluators from the sponsoring organization, such as the Delta Society or Therapy Dogs International (see page 92), evaluate the handler and dog. The evaluation typically consists of obedience and what a team might encounter on a visit, such as people in wheelchairs. Both members of the team must pass the evaluation. The evaluator must be certain both the volunteer and the animal interact well with each other, with other people, and with the surroundings. The volunteer handler must pass a written test. People of all ages, including youngsters in 4-H, participate in this rewarding activity.

Agility

Agility is a sport in which the handler directs his dog through a series of obstacles while the dog is off leash. The event is timed and the goal is to complete the course with the highest score or the quickest time possible. The obstacles are arranged in a random course but must be navigated in a set sequence. Certain obstacles, such as the pipe tunnel, are common to all events. The obstacles are designed for the dog's safety and for spectator appeal. It is an exciting event to watch as a dog enthusiastically races against the clock—leaping through jumps, climbing up and down obstacles, dashing through tunnels, and weaving between poles. Any fun-loving dog and person can participate in the sport. Agility requires nimbleness and dexterity. The dog must be healthy and willing to try new things. Weimaraners are fast and do fairly well; however, working dogs of medium build tend to be the most successful in competitions.

Many books and videos are available on agility. While your dog is still a puppy, you can begin teaching agility commands such as go, wait, left, and right. However, it is recommended that your dog not execute the jumps, except for very low ones, until he has stopped growing. Before participating in agility, have your veterinarian check your dog's health to make sure he is in good condition.

The American Kennel Club (AKC) sponsors Agility competitions. For more information, contact the AKC, at the address listed on page 92. Agility classes are offered in many urban areas and can be found by contacting local dog trainers. Because the equipment is large and expensive, joining a class is the best way to begin this sport and to practice.

Training your dog for tracking trials takes a lot of work, but it can be very rewarding.

Tracking

The Weimaraner has a sharp nose and performs well in tracking events if properly trained. In tracking events, a dog works on a harness and 40-foot (12 m) lead and must work at least 20 feet (6 m) in front of the handler. Tracking tests require the dog to follow a scent trail that has been aged over specified distances. The tracks are laid between a half-hour to five hours before the dog goes to work. The titles that can be earned are Tracking Dog (TD), Tracking Dog Excellent (TDX), and Variable Surface Tracking (VST). The titles must be earned sequentially. If a dog earns all three titles, he is a Champion Tracker (CT). Each test increases in complexity, including the age of the track, number of sharp turns, cross tracks, and more varying terrain, such as ditches, tall grass, and roads. Tracking Dog and Tracking Dog Excellent tests usually take place in fields and woods, while the VST tests a dog's tracking ability in more developed areas and on a minimum of three types of surfaces, such as concrete, grass, or sand. For more information about the rules and regulations for Tracking tests, contact the AKC (address on page 92).

Search and Rescue

Search and rescue is an intense volunteer activity requiring a large commitment of time and energy. Some search and rescue teams travel overseas to help find people injured in natural disasters. Most teams work with local law enforcement to help look for lost hikers, skiers, and children. Usually several teams of volunteers participate in a search and all help to locate the lost individual. Teams can be called to help with a search at any hour of the day or night. Search and rescue is exciting and rewarding, but can also be emotionally demanding, as not all victims are found alive. A strong camaraderie usually develops among teams of search and rescue dogs and handlers.

Although some of the earlier Weimaraners in the United States gained fame by finding lost people, the breed is not regularly used in search and rescue. Weimaraners perform well in fair weather; however, their short coat is less suitable for searches in cold weather. Members of search and rescue teams and their dogs must be in good physical condition and properly trained.

Flyball

Flyball is a fast-paced competitive sport that can be played outside and indoors (in gymnasiums). Teams composed of four dogs compete against each other in a relay race. Each dog races 51 feet (15.5 m) over four hurdles, then triggers a spring-loaded box to release a tennis ball. He catches the ball in his mouth, then sprints back over the hurdles, ideally without dropping the tennis ball. Back at the starting line, his teammates eagerly wait for their turn to run the same course. The first team to complete the course in the fastest time without any errors wins.

The height of the four hurdles is set 4 inches (10 cm) below the shoulder height of the shortest dog, with an 8-inch (20 cm) minimum. Because flyball requires jumping, a dog must be in good condition with sound joints. To learn more about flyball or to find a team in your area, contact the North American Flyball Association, at the address listed on page 92.

Weimaraner Club of America
Dorothy Derr, Corresponding Secretary
P.O. Box 2907
Muskogee, OK 74403
(918) 686-6027
www.weimclubamerica.org
Subscription information to the *Weimaraner Magazine* can be found at this site.

Weimaraner Rescue Club of America
Rebecca Weimer
(618) 236-1466

North American Versatile Hunting Dog Association (NAVHDA)
Box 520
Arlington Heights, IL 60006
(847) 253-6488

American Kennel Club
5580 Centerview Drive
Raleigh, NC 27606-3390

Therapy Dogs International
88 Bartely Road
Flanders, NJ 07836
(973) 252-9800

Delta Society
289 Perimeter Road East
Renton, WA 98055-1329
(800) 869-6898

North American Flyball Association
1002 East Samuel Avenue
Peoria Heights, IL 61614

National Animal Poison Control Center
(900) 680-0000
($20.00 for five minutes and $2.95 per minute thereafter)

Books

Alexander, Virginia and Isabell, Jackie. *Weimaraner Ways.* P.O. Box 1800, Germantown, MD 20875-1800: SunStar, 1998. (800) W-WEIMAR This 600-plus page book is the tour-de-force of books on Weimaraners and is an excellent source for fanciers who want to know more about the breed.

Hollings, Patsy. *The Essential Weimaraner.* New York: Howell Book House, 1996.

Nicholas, Anna Katherine. *Weimaraners.* Neptune, NJ: TFH Publications, 1983.

The more you learn about your dog, the better off you will both be.

Adult dog:
exercising of, 57
selection of, 31
Agility, 90
American Kennel Club,
9, 17
Aversion tool, 47

Barking, 57–58
Bathing, 62
Bed, 34
Behavior, 20–21
Behavior problems,
57–59
Bloat, 79–80
Blue, 15
Bones, 59–60
Breeders, 27
Breeding, 59
Breed standard, 11–15
Brushing, 62
Buying:
considerations before,
18–21, 25
first days after, 37–38
male vs. female,
22–23
sources, 27–28
two or more puppies,
23

Canine Good Citizen-
ship, 87
Children, 23, 40
Chocolate, 71
Collar, 34–35
"Come" command,
53–54
Commands. See also
specific command
tone of voice for, 46
types of, 50–54
Crate, 33–34, 42

Dental care, 63
Dog shows, 87
"Down" command, 52
"Drop it" command,
55

Ears:
breed standard, 13
care for, 63
Equipment:
for puppy, 33–37
for training, 49
Exercise, 18–19, 57
Eyes, 13–14, 39

Family, 18, 50
Feeding:
how much to give,
68–70
schedule for, 70–71
Field trials, 85
Fleas, 73–74
Food:
description of, 65
selection of, 67–68
specialty, 66–67
table scraps, 71
types of, 65–66

Gait, 13
Gender, 22–23
"Give" command, 55
Grooming, 62–63
Gun dog, 29–30

Health, 30–31
Health insurance, 73
Heartworms, 76–77
"Heel" command, 54
Height, 12, 22
Hip dysplasia, 27, 80–82
Hookworms, 75–76
House-training, 26,
42–43
Hunting, 11, 30, 86
Hypertrophic osteodys-
trophy, 82
Hypothyroidism, 82

Identification tag, 35
Immunizations, 77–79
Information resources,
92

Jumping, 58–59

Kennel, 60
Kennel cough, 78

Leash, 35
"Leave it" command, 54
Lifespan, 23, 60
Long hair, 15
Lyme disease, 75

Mange, 73
Nails, 62–63
Neutering, 59, 70
"No" command, 47, 51

Obedience training. See
Training
Obedience trials, 86–87
Origins, 5–8
"Out" command, 55

Pack behavior, 45–46
Papers, 30
Parasites:
external, 73–75
internal, 75–77
Pets, 23
Pet services, 25–26
Pet stores, 27–28
Pooper scooper, 35–36
Positive reinforcement,
47
Protectiveness, 21
Puppy:
age of, 28
characteristics of,
39–40
equipment for, 33–37
handling of, 40
health of, 30–31
house-training of, 26,
42–43
housing for, 33–34,
38–39
price of, 28
safety considerations,
39–40
show vs. pet quality,
28–29
socialization of, 55

time commitment for,
26
vaccinations for,
77–79

Rabies vaccine, 78
Registration, 30
"Release" command,
51–52
Roundworms, 75

Safety, 38–39
Search and rescue, 91
Senior dog:
caring for, 60–61
diet for, 66–67
Separation anxiety, 58
Shows, 87
"Sit" command, 52
Skin disorders, 82–83
Snake bite, 83
Socialization, 55
Spaying, 59, 70
"Stay" command, 53
Supplements, 71

Tapeworms, 76
Temperament, 13
Therapy dogs, 88, 90
Ticks, 74–75
Toys, 36–37, 59–60
Tracking, 91
Training:
consistency in, 48–49
description of, 19–20,
49–50
reasons for, 45–46
suggestions for, 46–47
when to begin, 46–47
Traveling, 40–41, 60
Trimming of nails, 62–63
Tumors, 83

Vaccines, 77–79
Veterinarian, 37

Water, 71
Weimaraner Club of
America, 11

About the Author

Susan Fox is a wildlife biologist and a freelance writer. She has written numerous books about the care of a variety of pets and is a columnist for a pet trade magazine.

Photo Credits

Norvia Behling: 2-3, 37, 48 (top), 56, 72, 80 (top); Rich Bergman: 84; Kent & Donna Dannen: 16, 69, 89 (top), 93; Tara Darling: 44, 49, 52, 53, 60, 61, 64, 68, 76, 77, 81 (top), 89 (bottom left), 92; Jim Elder: 13; Sue Fox: 80 (bottom); Harry Giglio: 41; Don & Dorothy Huffman: 21, 28, 29 (right), 81 (bottom); Philip & Arlene Marshrey: 4, 8, 9, 12, 20, 24, 29 (left), 36, 40, 48 (bottom), 89 (bottom right); Thomas B. Wilson: 32

Cover Photos

All cover photos by Paws for Pictures.

Important Note

This pet owner's guide tells the reader how to buy and care for Weimaraners. The author and the publisher consider it important to point out that the advice given in the book is meant primarily for normally developed puppies from a good breeder— that is, dogs of excellent physical health and good character.

Anyone who adopts a fully grown dog should be aware that the animal has already formed its basic impressions of human beings. The new owner should watch the animal carefully, including its behavior toward humans, and should meet the previous owner. If the dog comes from a shelter, it may be possible to get some information on the dog's background and peculiarities there. There are dogs that as a result of bad experiences with humans behave in an unnatural manner or may even bite. Only people that have experience with dogs should take in such an animal.

Caution is further advised in the association of children with dogs, in meetings with other dogs, and in exercising the dog without a leash.

Even well-behaved and carefully supervised dogs sometimes do damage to someone else's property or cause accidents. It is, therefore, in the owner's interest to be adequately insured against such eventualities, and we strongly urge all dog owners to purchase a liability policy that covers their dog.

Acknowledgments

The author would like to thank the following people for their help: Arlene Marshrey, Tom Wilson, Rebecca Weimer, Rick Van Etten (*Gun Dog* Magazine), Sarah Chvilick, Karen Sandvold, Judy Eddy, Matthew Kiesse, Sharon Sturm, Art Henderson, Jean Dodds, D.V.M., Judy Balog, and NAVHDA. The author would also like to thank Bob O'Sullivan, editor at Barron's Educational Series, Inc. for his patience and advice during this project.

A Word about Pronouns

Throughout this manual, for solely editorial reasons, we have used in some places the word "he" in situations where the text refers to either male or female Weimaraners. This was done simply to avoid the clumsiness of "he or she" in many places, and is in no way meant to lessen the importance of female pets in our lives.

All inquiries should be addressed to:
Barron's Educational Series, Inc.
250 Wireless Boulevard
Hauppauge, NY 11788
http://www.barronseduc.com

International Standard Book No. 0-7641-1322-4
Library of Congress Catalog Card No. 00-030357

Library of Congress Cataloging-in-Publication Data
Fox, Susan, 1962–
    Weimaraners / Susan Fox.
        p. cm.
    ISBN 0-7641-1322-4 (alk. paper)
    1. Weimaraner (Dog breed). I. Title.
SF429.W33 F68   2000
636.752—dc21   00-030357

Printed in Hong Kong
9 8 7 6 5 4 3 2 1